FRONTIERS IN

ARCHEOLOGY

FRONTIERS IN

ARCHEOLOGY

By ROBERT SILVERBERG

Maps by Dorothy de Fontaine

CHILTON BOOKS *Publishers* Philadelphia and New York
A DIVISION OF CHILTON COMPANY

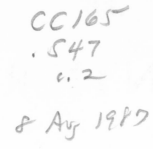

For JERRY MUNDIS

*who didn't have
many idle moments*

Contents

𝔊𝔊𝔊𝔊𝔊𝔊𝔊𝔊𝔊𝔊𝔊𝔊𝔊𝔊𝔊𝔊𝔊𝔊𝔊𝔊𝔊𝔊𝔊𝔊𝔊

Contents

Introduction

◨◨◨

AUSTEN HENRY LAYARD's busy spade lays bare the charred ruins of mighty Nineveh. Heinrich Schliemann drapes the necklace of a princess of Troy around the throat of his own youthful bride. Sir Arthur Evans uncovers the city of Minos, and the Labyrinth where Theseus slew the Minotaur. Howard Carter stands dumfounded amid the treasures of Tutankhamen. . . .

These were some of archeology's most glittering moments. As though by a flash of lightning and a peal of thunder, the earth opened and distant yesterdays stood revealed. The incomparable romance of these great archeological adventures has captivated readers for generations. There are those who come to popular books about archeology simply to follow the story of some determined man's struggle against the elements, the forces of confusion, and his own doubts. There are those who relish reading about the treasures the earth has yielded. And, I hope, there are some who draw from the romantic stories a knowledge of the underlying aim of archeology, which is not so much to fill the museums with works of art as it is to recapture and reconstruct the lost civilizations of the past in all their complexity. Whatever their motives, at any rate, the readers abound.

And so the stories of Layard and Schliemann, of Evans and Carter, of Koldewey at Babylon and Mouhot at Angkor and Stephens amid the jungle cities of the Maya, have become twice-told tales. I am among the retellers myself, in two earlier books: *Lost Cities and Vanished Civilizations* (1962) and *Empires in the Dust* (1963).

The stories of the archeological pioneers never lose their luster in these repeated retellings. But they *were* pioneers, and in re-counting the adventures of a Layard it should not be forgotten that the work of archeology is far from finished. Splendid new accomplishments are in the making, and news of them fills the professional journals of archeology, destined to filter into more popular form in the fullness of time. Though archeology has lost some of the romance it had in the heroic days of the nine-teenth century, it has gained in precision. By today's standards Layard, who began excavating the Assyrian mounds in 1845, was hopelessly inept. If he were to publish his findings in *Antiquity* or *The Journal of Near Eastern Studies* today, the pro-fessionals would flay him without mercy for his neglect of the most elementary techniques. That is the peril of pioneering; first come the heroic figures, then the body of technique.

We respect the Layards for their triumphs over obstacles, and we admire them for their dash and vigor. But it is useful to consider some of the accomplishments of more recent archeolo-gists. Layard and Schliemann were archeologists of the Neo-lithic age, so to speak. Evans, though he died only a generation ago, was a figure out of the dawn of scientific archeology, un-der heavy attack today for some of his practices. Carter, a mod-ern archeologist of the finest kind, found Tutankhamen in 1922 —and 1922, that year of crystal radios, flimsy airplanes, the Model T, and gaslit houses, was a long time ago.

So this book looks toward the frontiers of archeology: the work done in the past thirty or forty years, and most particularly in the years since the end of World War II. It does not pretend to be a report on what is happening at the present instant. The six archeological stories in this book have all reached, if not a conclusion, at least enough of a climax so that it does not seem premature to write about them. They are recent but not raw. Kathleen Kenyon ended her work at Jericho in 1958; Claude Schaeffer is no longer digging at Ras Shamra; Easter Island at the moment is between expeditions. The work con-tinues at Zimbabwe, in Mexico, and at the capital of the Shang Dynasty, but the picture as it now stands is clear enough to be offered, whatever later modifications may appear notwithstand-ing.

The technique of these archeologists of today's frontier would bedazzle the pioneers. The decaying atoms of radioactive carbon-14 help in determining the age of a site; aerial photography identifies ruins not visible from the ground; the spectrometer and the chromatograph and other arcane devices aid in opening the doors of the past. Though the basic procedure has remained the same throughout this century—careful digging, identification of each stratum—the tools are new and often startling. So are the results.

The narratives of this book may not match in surface gleam the tales of the pioneers. The glamor is generally more subtle these days. The flamboyance of a Schliemann has given way to the methodical expertise of a Kathleen Kenyon. But archeology remains exciting, even if the excitement is of a different kind. I hope some of that excitement is transmitted here.

ROBERT SILVERBERG

FRONTIERS IN

ARCHEOLOGY

The spelling of the word "archeology" throughout this book is in accordance with modern American usage. The author, who prefers the traditional spelling, has been gracious enough to accede to the publisher's wishes.

But the iniquity of oblivion blindely scattereth her poppy, and deals with the memory of men without distinction to merit of perpetuity. Who can but pity the founder of the Pyramids? Herostratus *lives that burnt the Temple of* Diana; *he is almost lost that built it; Time hath spared the Epitaph of* Adrians *horse, confounded that of himself. In vain we compute our felicities by the advantage of our good names, since bad have equall duratations; and* Thersites *is like to live as long as* Agamemnon. *Who knows whether the best of men be known? or whether there be not more remarkable persons forgot than any that stand remembred in the known account of time?*

Sir Thomas Browne
Hydriotaphia

One

Jericho: The Oldest City

ABOUT thirty-two centuries ago, a wandering Semitic tribe we call the Israelites departed from Egypt and made its way northward toward the land of Canaan. We have a chronicle of that journey, written some centuries after the fact but probably fairly reliable. It tells us how the Israelites passed over the River Jordan, "and encamped in Gilgal, in the east border of Jericho."

The Jordan flows from north to south, ending in the salty wastes of the Dead Sea. Jericho was then and is now a city at the northern end of the Dead Sea, controlling the narrow valley that leads onward to fertile country. The Israelites, approaching from the south and the east, had wandered long enough in the desert; now they yearned to enter Canaan, and that meant conquering Jericho.

The story is a familiar one. The Old Testament tells us of Joshua's scheme of challenging Jericho's mighty walls with trumpets and horns:

So the people shouted when the priests blew with the trumpets: and it came to pass, when the people heard the sound of the trumpet, and the people shouted with a great shout, that the wall fell down flat, so that the people went up into the city, every man straight before him, and they took the city.

And they utterly destroyed all that was in the city, both man and woman, young and old, and ox, and sheep, and ass, with the edge of the sword. . . .

And they burnt the city with fire, and all that was therein.

When archeology first became a popular pastime in the nineteenth century, the motivating interest of many archeologists was

[1]

to confirm—if possible—the stories of the Bible. Partly this was a matter of religious zeal, but it also happened that the scriptures were practically the only available chronicle of historical events in the ancient Near East. The copious documents of Egypt and Mesopotamia were still indecipherable, and the only other guides to past events were the writings of such early historians as Herodotus and Diodorus Siculus. So the archeologists who worked in Egypt and Palestine and Mesopotamia took as their starting point the quest to match the realities of their sites to the narratives of the Bible.

Jericho, with its flattened walls, was an obvious target—especially since the old name had survived. The modern town of Jericho is the lowest-lying settlement on earth: 840 feet below sea level, at the foot of the long slope down from the highlands on which Jerusalem sits. The Jordan has carved a deep gash into this slope; to one side of the valley lies rocky Israel with its cultivated hillsides, to the other is the sprawling grassland of the Kingdom of Jordan, stretching eastward to the parched Syrian Desert.

Kathleen M. Kenyon, the modern excavator of Jericho, has written of traveling the winding road from Jerusalem to Jericho:

As the road descends, gray hills with their terraced fields and scattering of olive trees are left behind. Here are glaring slopes too waterless to be cultivated, fit only for flocks of goats and sheep that subsist on vegetation which comes up after the winter rains. Suddenly there appears the flat plain of Jericho, the bottom of a great rift through which the River Jordan coils to lose itself in the Dead Sea. The center of the plain is a fantastic badlands where the river has twisted its channel between slimy white mounds. This landscape is glaring white in the sunshine and inexpressibly barren.

An oasis in this blackness harbors modern Jericho. Groves of banana trees and palms surround it. The cool, sweet flow of a spring called Elisha's Fountain, northwest of the town, makes the fields fertile. And besides this spring, about a mile from the modern town, stands a mud-colored mound called Tell es-Sultan —the site of the city Joshua conquered.

In the Near East, a *tell* is an artificial mound created by the building of one settlement over another, layer upon layer. Some tells represent thousands of years of consecutive occupation, broken by repeated intervals of desolation and abandonment. They are complex sandwiches of ruins, formed as each new set of inhabitants builds upon the rubble of the last dwellers.

By the middle of the nineteenth century, the nature of the tells was understood, and archeologists were digging into them with cheerful vigor. The shining example of Austen Henry Layard, who had won fame, fortune, and a seat in Parliament by unearthing the mound-covered cities of Assyria, was before everyone's eyes. A young ordnance officer named Charles Warren had read Layard's best-selling books and probably had some hope of emulating his career. When the Palestine Exploration Fund was established in England in 1865, chiefly for the purpose of reconnoitering the Biblical sites, Warren volunteered for service.

He dug for a while at Jerusalem; then, in search of sculpture and reliefs of the sort that had made Layard an internationally known figure, he tackled Tell es-Sultan. But his primitive archeological technique was foiled by the mud-brick construction of the buildings on the mound. He was stymied, as Layard had been at Babylon, by his inability to distinguish debris from building walls, and he had to retreat in dismay. In his book of 1876, *Underground Jerusalem,* Warren wrote of his Jericho expedition in a tone of regret:

Grand visions of what existed in the interior [of Tell es-Sultan] dimly shadowed themselves forth and excluded every other view: the colossal figures which emanated from my excited imagination far exceeded anything obtained from Nineveh by Layard. And now that the dream of bringing them to England is over, now that this draw in the lottery of life is a blank, can I say they were not met with, that others do not yet exist within those mounds? In truth, I cannot. In excavating those remains of a bygone race, we were groping in a land of shadows and phantoms; ever and anon, as the pick opened up the soil, the half-light revealed to us objects which evaded our grasp, which, on being brought to the strong daylight, vanished from view and returned into the dust from which they were constructed. The very bricks ceased to exist as bricks when exposed to the air. It cannot, then, be said that in these mounds, so thoroughly ripped open, there are not monuments of the greatest importance yet

[3]

existing, but if so, they must be obtained in some special manner, for a few seconds sufficed to take away their appearance and leave but a yellow marly clay.

Warren was naïve but candid: he was looking for treasure. During the half century that followed, the goals of archeology shifted, and the ultimate aim became not plunder but knowledge, the abstract, unprofitable resurrection of the life and times of dead civilizations. Such great archeologists as William Matthew Flinders Petrie (1853–1942) evolved methods of peeling away a mound layer by layer, recording all that was in one stratum before unearthing the next. When the next archeologists came to Jericho, they were men of this new persuasion.

From 1907 to 1909 a joint German-Austrian expedition, led by Ernst Sellin and Karl Watzinger, worked there. Their excavation report, issued in 1913, was a model of its type. They had discovered two amazing rings of fortification, which they documented with plans and photographs. The massive inner wall, a twelve-foot thickness of sun-dried bricks, surrounded the ridge of the hill. About ten feet beyond it, at the foot of the hill, ran a six-foot-thick brick outer wall, nearly thirty feet high. With perhaps forgivable enthusiasm, Sellin and Watzinger announced that they had found *the* walls of Jericho.

Comparative chronology was still in its developmental state. Flinders Petrie and his colleagues had begun to work out a scheme for the Near East based on the changing types of pottery found in the mounds—for pottery is practically indestructible once it has reached the fragmentary potsherd form, and ancient potters tended to use one style in one place for long periods of time. The "pottery calendar" did not give dates for each successive type, but it did provide a rough clue to the relative age of a site, and where documents could be deciphered it even offered absolute dating. Sellin and Watzinger, however, preferred their own system of chronology to the one being worked out by the British, and that led to trouble.

The thick inner, upper wall, they said, was the work of Hiel the Bethelite, who lived about 880 B.C. According to the Bible, Joshua had declared, "Cursed be the man before the Lord, that riseth up and buildeth this city, Jericho." The site remained a wasteland until the time of King Ahab, when Hiel dared to build there, and suffered the loss of his eldest and youngest sons for violating Joshua's curse. As for the outer wall, Sellin and Watzinger announced that it was the veritable wall of Joshua's time, which the Israelites had breached about 1200 B.C.

These opinions were immediately challenged, and a noisy controversy followed. It remained for later archeologists to show that the so-called wall of Hiel had been built no later than the seventeenth century B.C. while the wall allegedly destroyed by Joshua was some centuries older than that, dating to the Early Bronze Age. The German-Austrian expedition had been working in strata that were centuries old when the Israelites began their march into the Promised Land.

The onset of World War I interrupted archeological work in the Near East. After the war, Great Britain took control of Palestine by mandate of the League of Nations, and a new era in Biblical archeology began. John Garstang of the University of Liverpool, who had done important work on the Hittite civilization * in the early years of the century, became head of the Department of Antiquities in the mandated territory in 1920. For the next fifteen years, until political disorder in Palestine interfered with excavation, British archeologists worked at many Biblical sites.

Garstang himself investigated Jericho from 1930 to 1936, naturally devoting much of his attention to the problem of the walls. He agreed that the inner wall was more recent than the outer one. His precise approach revealed the holocaust that the ancient city must have suffered: "The space between the two walls is filled with fragments and rubble," he wrote. "There are clear traces of a tremendous fire, compact masses of blackened bricks, cracked stones, charred wood, and ashes. Along the walls the houses have been burned to the ground and their roofs have crashed on top of them." The inner wall, which Sellin and Watzinger had ascribed to Hiel the Bethelite, was actually, according to Garstang, the wall of Joshua's conquest. The outer wall he recognized as dating from some much more remote period.

* See my *Empires in the Dust* (Chilton, 1963), pp. 52–90.

Garstang's speculations about the walls were of minor importance in comparison to his actual accomplishments at the site. He drove meticulous trenches deep into Tell es-Sultan, penetrating the Bronze Age layers and going beneath them to strata of a time when men had used chipped flints as tools. His discovery of a Neolithic, or New Stone Age, layer at the bottom of the Jericho sandwich startled the world of archeology. It appeared that Tell es-Sultan had been continuously inhabited for more than eight thousand years, which if true made it one of the most important sites in the Near East. None of the cities of Egypt or Mesopotamia appeared to be older than six thousand years.

The turmoil of the war years prevented any further work in Palestine, and after the war the period of uncertainty that led to the birth of the state of Israel also kept archeologists away. The next expedition that came to Jericho did not dig at Tell es-Sultan but concentrated instead on New Testament Jericho, a nearby ruin built in Roman times. This had been the winter capital of Herod the Great, and Christ had stopped there on his way to Jerusalem and the Crucifixion. The American School of Oriental Research in Jerusalem sponsored this excavation, which began in January, 1950, under the direction of James L. Kelso of the Pittsburgh-Xenia Theological Seminary.

Dr. Kelso's work was valuable in uncovering the ruins of a short-lived city of Christ's time, but it did not answer the larger questions posed by the much more ancient mound of Tell es-Sultan a mile and three quarters to the east. The American School of Oriental Research wished to reopen the dig there, too, and found a willing collaborator in the British School of Archaeology in Jerusalem. The partition of Palestine had placed Jericho in the Kingdom of Jordan, but British civil servants were still employed there, and Jordan's Director or Antiquities, G. Lankester Harding, readily granted permission for the work. (Harding was dismissed in 1956 during a general purge of Jordan's British officials.)

The complex negotiations that led to the renewal of work at Jericho were the responsibility of Kathleen Kenyon, who in 1951 became director of the British School of Archaeology in Jerusalem. Miss Kenyon, the daughter of a famous archeologist and Biblical scholar, had begun her own career at the age of twenty-three, in 1929, when she took part in excavations at the site of Zimbabwe in Southern Rhodesia. After extensive work in England and the Near East, she became a specialist in the archeology of Palestine and late in 1951 began to assemble her Jericho expedition.

She pitched camp beside Elisha's Fountain in January, 1952, with a staff of some twenty workers. A. Douglas Tushingham of the American School served as assistant director. The first task was to survey the mound and get perspective on the many layers of occupation. The technique for this has become fairly standard since Flinders Petrie's day, and since the Kenyon approach was a model of its sort, it deserves a close look.

A stratification survey begins with a trial trench cut sharply through an entire mound from top to bottom. That exposes all the walls and occupation levels along a vertical face. Each layer of soil is identified and traced, and the distinctions between layers are rigorously followed throughout the excavation. One of Miss Kenyon's maps of Jericho bristles with a host of labeled strata: "Grey soil with stones and bricks," "fine brown soil and horizontal striations," "rubbly to clayey with horizontal ash streaks," and so on.

The trial trench is the key to all that follows. To quote Miss Kenyon:

When excavation is begun in any one area, the workmen start to remove the soil, and the supervisor records a description of it in his notebook, for instance "Level I. Grey rubbly soil." All finds, pottery, flints, bones, are put into a container which is labelled with the designation of the area (Trench I, Square D, and so on) and the description and number of the layer. As soon as there is a change in the soil, and the clearance of the upper layer is completed, a new entry is made in the notebook, for instance "Level II. Compact brown soil," and the finds are put into a separate container, appropriately labelled. At the end of the day, the finds are all taken down to the dig headquarters, and next day they are washed (unless they are too fragile) and given a preliminary sorting to eliminate the objects of no significance and to make a first identification of the period. They are then marked, tied up in bags or boxes, and stored for more detailed examination and recording when all the material of one phase can be assembled together.

[7]

Miss Kenyon did not attempt a total excavation of Jericho. Excavation means destruction, and a full-scale leveling of the nine-acre mound not only would have required a lifetime but would have obliterated it for future workers. Since there is steady progress in the techniques of archeology, field workers customarily leave a substantial section of each site for those who follow after. This was not always the practice, and many sites were irretrievably damaged by well-meaning but unschooled pioneers in the last century. Charles Warren, when he dug at Jericho in 1867, had the good sense to quit when he saw that he was ruining all that he uncovered, but others persisted, to the everlasting regret of later archeologists.

The aspects of Jericho that interested Miss Kenyon were its alpha and omega: the Neolithic site discovered by Garstang and the Biblical-era Jericho destroyed by Joshua. She intended to make a careful study of the strata that came between, of course, but they were not her primary interests. The obvious starting point for examination of the earliest levels was Garstang's shaft on the northeast side of the tell. He had sunk a pit to the Neolithic levels that was about six feet by nine at its lowest point. This shaft was still in good shape, sixteen years after the end of Garstang's work, and needed only minor clearing before the Kenyon expedition could enter it. Miss Kenyon also drove a trial trench on the west side of the tell, where she found that the Neolithic levels lay only four feet below the surface, most of the more recent deposits having weathered away.

The information produced by these early explorations led her to start additional trenches at the north and south ends of the tell. In each of her three shafts, and in the one inherited from Garstang, the aim was to dig down to bedrock or to virgin soil, thus reaching the point where human occupation began.

Trench I, on the western side of the mound, produced a problem and a surprise. Early in 1953, at the outset of the second season of work, the excavators laid bare a portion of a human skull as they carried this trench downward. It was a temptation to expose it completely and see if it led the way to some new discovery. "But," as Miss Kenyon observed, "one never goes burrowing about an ancient site just to remove things. Maintaining a straight vertical edge on an excavation, so that layers marking successive settlements may be recorded accurately, is a cardinal rule of modern archeology. So there we left it."

The tantalizing skull remained partly visible for most of the 1953 season, jutting from a layer thought to be at least seven thousand years old. Miss Kenyon grudgingly admitted that it might be considered "something of a special case," and so, once the stratification charts had been drawn, she gave permission for the skull's removal. She asked the site supervisor, Peter Parr, to make as small a hole as possible in the side of the trench.

Later that day, Parr reported that the skull seemed to be coated with a layer of clay. At nightfall he produced an astonishing object. The skull, of Neolithic age, was covered with plaster molded into human features. Features had been lovingly modeled, the ears, eyebrows, mouth, and cheeks all done with extreme delicacy. The eyes were inset segments of shell, with a vertical slit between to represent the pupil. The folds of the eyelid, the nostrils, the prim line of the mouth, and other touches made the skull not a stylized and impersonal mask but a vivid and faithful depiction of what must have been its owner's features in life. "Here was a missing link so unexpected that it had never been missed!" Kathleen Kenyon wrote. "No archeologist had even guessed at the existence of such a work of art, foreshadowing the great traditions of Mesopotamia, Egypt, and ancient Greece. We realized with a thrill of discovery that we were looking at the portrait of a man who lived and died more than 7,000 years ago."

Two more skulls were visible in the opening from which the first had been removed. When these were taken out, three more could be seen. A seventh lay behind them. Though summer's blazing heat was upon the archeologists, and the season's dig should have been terminated, they worked on, with their bags already packed, to clear these skulls. It was a taxing operation; the fragile skulls were packed in a compact heap, and it took five days to extract them all.

An incredible portrait gallery lay before them. Some of the skulls still had patches of paint; one was a warm flesh color all over. Nothing had prepared the archeologists for the discovery of such elegant works of art in the Stone Age layers of Jericho. But what were they? Why had craftsmen of that distant era so deftly modeled portraits in plaster over human skulls?

Contemporary anthropologists had reported a similar modeling of features on skulls among the Sipek River head-hunters of New Guinea. Some of these decorated skulls were those of enemies, others of revered tribal ancestors. Kathleen Kenyon inclines toward the theory that the Jericho skulls are ancestral portraits, probably sacred objects of some cult of the dead. But the contrary idea, that they could be the remains of vanquished foes, kept as trophies of battle, has its adherents too.

Season after season the Jericho excavation continued. The work was slowed by the necessity to haul away the earth dumped on the site by Garstang and earlier archeologists, for it had not always been possible for Miss Kenyon's predecessors to dump their soil clear of the mound as they dug. The 1954 season produced a pleasant moment when the archeologists working at the south end of the tell found themselves in a pit with modern filling unrecorded by Garstang or the German-Austrian excavators. It turned out to be one of the shafts sunk by Charles Warren in 1867. He had driven his trench twenty feet down, into the town wall of an Early Bronze Age settlement, but he had failed to recognize the nature of his find and had closed the shaft.

Nothing that emerged in the five seasons after 1953 had the romantic appeal and headline-getting value of the seven portrait skulls. But as the Kenyon expedition peeled away the many levels of Jericho, an enormously significant archeological story was revealed in detail. From the mound of Tell es-Sultan came the biography of the oldest known city of mankind.

The lowest levels were Neolithic. They dated from a time when the use of metals was unknown, when even pottery, that universal of Near Eastern sites, had not yet been developed. Flint knives, borers, scrapers, arrowheads, and sickles abounded. There were stone querns for grinding corn, tools of bone, hammers and pestles of stones other than flint.

The carbon-14 method supplies dates for Neolithic Jericho. This remarkable technique developed by Dr. Willard F. Libby in the late 1940's, provides strikingly accurate dates by measuring the radioactive decay of an isotope of carbon found in all living organisms. At death, the intake of carbon-14 ceases, and since its breakdown proceeds at a fixed rate, organic matter can be dated by analyzing the quantity of the isotope it contains.

At Jericho, charcoal fragments found in one of the higher levels of the Neolithic zone gave carbon-14 dates of about 5850 B.C. and 6250 B.C. A lower level produced a date of about 6800 B.C. Nor was this the bottom of the mound, though no datable material could be found in lower strata. The results showed continuous occupation of Jericho for at least nine thousand years, with the possibility of even greater antiquity than that.

These dates are nothing very amazing in the over-all story of man. The cave paintings of France are at least three times as old as the earliest levels of Jericho. Those paintings were made by tribesmen of a nomadic hunting and food-gathering culture, though, who had no knowledge of agriculture, of architecture, of any of the functions of settled civilization. Their community structure was probably no more than a family or tribal one, held together by the flimsiest of bonds.

But Jericho was a *town,* nine thousand years ago. Fifty centuries before the Pyramids rose in Egypt, a large fortified community existed in the valley of the Jordan, raising crops and domesticated animals. At that incredibly early date, when virtually all the world was a hunting ground for simple nomads, Jericho was a self-sufficient and fully organized settlement of cooperating citizens.

The size of Neolithic Jericho indicates how advanced its people were. It was a goodly village surrounded by massive walls and covering at least eight acres. Its population may have been as much as three thousand. The defensive wall, first uncovered in 1952, consisted of large crude stones taken from the beds of streams about half a mile away. Miss Kenyon found this wall surviving to a height of more than eight feet, and stretches of it sixty and seventy feet long were discovered. The wall evidently had collapsed and had been rebuilt, but after a second collapse a new wall had been erected in front of the old, rising on the tumbled debris. On the inner side of the wall, an even more remarkable structure was unearthed: a ponderous circular stone tower, almost thirty feet in diameter, pierced by a sloping staircase whose stone steps had been carefully squared and dressed.

Such elaborate fortifications amazed the excavators, who found it hard to believe that they could be eight or nine thousand years old. Certainly the community that built them must have been well organized, with purposeful leadership and a host of skilled craftsmen. Only a well-developed system of agriculture could possibly have supported this ambitious program of public works, since a community in which every man must scrabble for food to keep away starvation has no time to build walls and towers. The fertility of Jericho's oasis must have been important in fostering this agriculture, though it would have been necessary for the ancient farmers to devise a network of irrigation channels in order to raise crops sufficient to keep so large a village fed. This, too, is testimony to the precocious development of Jericho.

It could only have been an interconnected chain of circumstances that permitted the Jericho settlement to evolve. A good location, a dependable source of water, intelligent leadership, the willingness to join in common endeavors, the creation of irrigation works, the raising of generous crops—all these were necessary before the walled city could take form. Kathleen Kenyon does not think Jericho was unique; almost certainly it was one of a number of towns that made the break-through from food gathering to food producing sometime after 10,000 B.C. and went on to a robust expansion. But it happens that Jericho is the only Neolithic village that has been excavated up till now, which is why it can be considered the world's oldest town.

The archeologists were able to distinguish two separate levels of Neolithic occupation. One level, ranging in age from 7,500 to 8,500 years, had houses with good-sized rooms arranged around central courtyards, a pattern still generally favored in that part of the world. The courtyards must have been family gathering places, and they also served as kitchens, for the archeologists found successions of hearths in them. Evidently whenever the layers of ashes and grease became unmanageable, the townspeople simply laid down a new clay surface and began anew. The courtyard floors thus consisted of innumerable layers of cooking refuse separated by thin clay pavements.

The houses were of sun-dried brick set in a clay mortar, although stone was used to some extent in the foundations. The room floors were of clay, surfaced with fine plaster of a red or cream color that could be burnished to a high polish. The plaster surface made a concave junction with the walls, no doubt to keep dust and debris from accumulating in the corners of the rooms. "The whole impression of the houses is that of good, solid, well-planned lay-out," Kathleen Kenyon wrote.

There is even evidence of a considerable degree of comfort, for we have found that the floors of several of the rooms were covered by rush mats. These survive only as a thin white film, but the texture of the rushes which made them, and the weave of the mats is perfectly clear. One was apparently rectangular, and there are four examples of round mats of varying sizes. One of these even shows the track of a white ant which ate its way across it.

This was a pre-pottery culture; the villagers had learned to use clay in their buildings and in floor plasterings, but had not yet attained the use of the kiln, which imparts hardness to clay vessels. Their dishes and bowls were fashioned from soft polished limestone. Doubtless they also made containers of skins and wood, but these have perished.

This culture—what Kathleen Kenyon refers to as "the people of the plaster-floor phase"—was responsible for the extraordinary coated skulls discovered during the 1953 season. The skulls testify to the artistic and perhaps the religious aspects of life in plaster-floor times. Small ax-shaped amulets of green stone seem to have been religious objects as well, since they have no apparent functional purpose. (Though they appear to be miniature axes, their shape is puzzling in origin, because the plaster-floor people did not have any such heavy tools as axes, adzes, picks, or hoes.)

Another religious element of the plaster-floor phase was a room in one house that quite likely was a shrine. In a niche of the end wall a chipped oval stone of volcanic rock stood upright on a rough stone pedestal. "There can be little doubt that we have here a cult object," Miss Kenyon reported, "a recognition that there was a supernatural force which could be anonymously represented in this way." Not far from this room, which perhaps was a family chapel, the excavators found a larger building that they tentatively identified as a temple. It had a central rectangular room of large size, with a small basin neatly positioned at its center. Walls, floor, and basin all were covered with fine, highly polished plaster, and about the basin itself the plaster showed scorching, as if some ceremonial fire had been maintained there.

The famous Jericho skulls were found beneath the plastered floor of another house. In 1956, two more skulls were found ten feet away under the same floor. They lay in the debris of an earlier house, probably the one in which they had been kept as treasures. When the floor of this lower house was opened, it was found to hide some thirty skeletons, tightly packed into a small area. The skulls had been removed from several of the skeletons. Though burials were found beneath the floors of many buildings in the Neolithic levels—floor burial was a widespread custom in much of the ancient Near East—this was the only mass grave, and the only one in which detached skulls were found. Miss Kenyon suggested that these might have been the victims of some great massacre, or perhaps the remains of vanquished marauders. Since many of the skeletons of the other burials were lacking the skulls, she offered the hypothesis that a skull cult was general in Neolithic Jericho, and that the skulls of loved ones were removed after death, modeled with plaster to simulate the features of the departed, and placed in a community graveyard which has not yet been discovered.

As the archeologists worked on this Neolithic zone, with its striking skulls, its awesome walls, and its impressive circular tower, it became apparent by 1956 that a still older phase lay beneath. The floors on this level were of mud and not plaster; the buildings were round in plan, with curved walls made of curious bricks whose bases were flat and whose upper surfaces were curved in a hog-back shape. A substantial gap in the strata separated this "hog-back-brick phase" from the plaster-floor phase above it. The gap was marked by deposits of silt and gravel laid down by a stream that had flooded through the town. Obviously Jericho had been abandoned by the hog-back-brick people and the settlement left to the mercy of the elements for a period that may have been only three years or perhaps much more, before the plaster-floor people began to build on the crumbling foundations of their predecessors.

The hog-back-brick people, with their beehive houses and their mud floors, must certainly have been a different group from the plaster-floor folk. Their culture was distinct in every way: the shape of grinding stones and bowls, the design of flint tools, the extensive use of wood in architecture, the layout of the streets. They, too, fashioned amulets of green stone, but of a different shape. Like the plaster-floor people, they seem to have had a cult of skulls, however. The archeologists found a great many skulls separate from their skeletons and arranged in close-packed groups, facing inward in one case, all looking in the same direction in another.

These people were the founders of Jericho. How long they may have lived in the valley of the Jordan as wanderers and seed gatherers is unknown, but perhaps as early as 8000 B.C. they began to come together, as villagers and farmers, and within a thousand years had built a full-scale walled town. The huge walls, no doubt, were intended as a defense against the plaster-floor folk, who could well have been the inhabitants of some nearby Palestinian settlement.

Then, possibly about 6500 B.C., the hog-back-brick people were overwhelmed by their enemies. Jericho was destroyed. After some years of neglect, the plaster-floor people took possession of the ruined city and its life-giving spring. They arrived with a fully developed culture of their own, since its earliest stages at Jericho are already quite sophisticated. Their occupation of Jericho was a lengthy one, long enough to raise a mound forty-five feet high, in which fourteen successive stages of development could be traced.

All this was a revelation to archeologists. No one had expected to find Neolithic settlements of such complexity that dated back eight thousand years and more. It had previously been thought that the town-building stage had not been reached until the fourth millennium B.C. in southern Mesopotamia, and somewhat later in other regions of the Near East. The established ideas about the beginnings of settled life had to be substantially revised.

Why had Jericho—and its still-unknown neighbors—blossomed so early?

One explanation that is widely accepted links Jericho's rise to the glacial period. Repeatedly, over the last million and a half years, world-wide dips in mean temperature have resulted in ice ages that covered the temperate zones with a glacial sheath. The chilling process, though, produced only heavy rain in the tropics—a "pluvial" age that transformed deserts into gardens. The last of these glacial-pluvial periods ended about 10,000 B.C., from which time there has been a steady rise in temperatures.

In the Near East, the pluvial age may have stimulated the development of agriculture in former desert regions. As the centuries passed, and these regions returned to their old aridity, life must have become harsh for these premature farmers, and finally a stage was reached where their simple methods of agriculture could no longer contend with the growing dryness.

The farming settlements of the dawn collapsed. In their place came towns of a more modest sort, whose inhabitants adjusted to their reduced circumstances. At Jericho, the time of reckoning for the plaster-floor people may have come about 5000 B.C. They abandoned their town and sought greener fields elsewhere.

Some years later, newcomers arrived. They were makers of fine pottery decorated with polished patterns, red diamonds and triangles on a cream-colored background. They seem to have been squatters who camped on the rubble-filled ruins of the plaster-floor people's abandoned houses. They built no houses of their own, left the city wall in its ruined state, and scratched out a livelihood of meager crops and skimpy harvests. The chief evidence of their presence is the enormous quantity of broken pottery that they scattered about, the oldest pottery to be found on the Jericho site.

The impression that their culture was a scanty one is dispelled only by a group of finds made by the Garstang expedition and thought to be the work of these people (who are called the "Pottery Neolithic A" people in the Kenyon terminology). Garstang uncovered three plaster statues, nearly life-size. They were badly damaged, and only the male figure still had its head. This portrait head resembled the much more ancient plastered skulls in several respects: the features were molded from plaster, and the eyes were represented by shells. Brown paint indicated the hair and beard. Though these figures are not clearly the breathtaking objects that the plastered skulls are, they indicate some artistic and possibly religious impulses among the Pottery Neolithic A dwellers.

The accumulation of potsherds of the A type shows that these people must have remained at Jericho a considerable time, a few centuries, perhaps. But, as Kathleen Kenyon notes, "in all respects they remain somewhat shadowy." Their successors, the Pottery Neolithic B people, replaced them about 4750 B.C.

There is no carbon-14 date from Jericho to support this guess. But the B type of Jericho pottery is clearly related to other pottery that was widespread in Syria and Palestine at the same time, and from another site comes a carbon-14 date of c. 4750 B.C. that probably is valid for most of the region that produced this sort of ware. Instead of decorating their pottery with red patterns, the B people often incised their designs into the clay. The effect is not as attractive as in the A pottery, but the ware is much more capably made, harder, better fired, with less straw mixed with the clay.

The Neolithic Pottery B people's houses suffered badly at the hands of later inhabitants of Jericho, who plundered them of bricks. Scarcely more than the foundations remain. They are marked by bricks of a distinct kind, which the excavators termed "bun-shaped." Flat on bottom, curved above, and round in outline, they are altogether different from the earlier bricks of the two pre-pottery cultures and from the later Bronze Age bricks.

These B people seem not to have had a very elaborate culture, judging from what little has survived of their stratum. They departed; and a gap of many centuries exists in the chronological record of Tell es-Sultan after them. At least three hundred years passed, possibly much more. Jericho's Neolithic period ended about 4000 B.C., and the next level of occupation can be dated to about 3200 B.C.

During those missing centuries, much was happening in the world beyond Jericho. The scattered villages of Egypt were being welded into a single kingdom, and the scribes of Sumer were devising their wedge-shaped way of writing on clay tablets. Men were making their first attempts to utilize such metals as bronze. New types of pottery were conceived, and their use spread through the Near East.

The world had changed considerably by the time new dwellers settled permanently at Jericho. Fugitive bands of nomads may have occupied the mound for brief periods, but they left no record of their presence. By 3200 B.C., though, a phase that Miss Kenyon terms the Proto-Urban Age had begun, and the rebuilding of the already ancient site of Jericho got under way.

These people were tomb builders. Instead of burying their dead beneath the floors of their homes, they interred them in deep round-walled shafts sunk into the rock of the hills north of the town. One noteworthy tomb of this period, with a carbon-14 date of 3260 B.C. ± 110 years, contained 113 skulls set in a circle facing the center of the tomb, where a cremation pile of burned bones was heaped. The archeologists speculated that this was a secondary burial, since the dead had been previously exposed until the bones of the skeletons had separated; then all were collected, taken to this burial place, and cremated but for the skulls. It is interesting to note the persistence of the skull cult at Jericho over thousands of years, even with great gaps in the sequence of occupation.

Not much is known about these tomb builders aside from their unusual funeral customs. Probably Palestine was in a state of flux, with tribes coming and going and new ideas flooding across the land out of the by now highly developed cultures of Egypt and Sumer. By 2900 B.C., the Bronze Age seems to have reached Jericho, which once had been in the vanguard of progress but now was merely a provincial backwater.

The phase kown as the Early Bronze Age lasted six centuries at Jericho. After seven seasons of excavation, though, Kathleen Kenyon could only describe her information about this period as "disjointed." Much of the level had been stripped away by erosion and by later inhabitants of the site, while the Austro-German excavations early in this century had cut a great trench through it. But what did remain for the Kenyon group to study, in the Early Bronze Age level, was the cultural manifestation most closely associated with the traditional Jericho: walls.

No one had built walls at Jericho for two thousand years, but the Early Bronze Age people evidently felt that they had something worth protecting. Their walls, which do not follow the lines of the Neolithic defenses, were strong and extensive and must have served them in good stead in this time of political uncertainty. The Kenyon group, patiently plotting a plan of a maze of walls so intricate as to bedazzle a layman, concluded that between 2900 and 2300 B.C. the defenses of Jericho were altered and rebuilt at least sixteen times. Disentangling this sequence, naturally, was a formidable task. As Miss Kenyon explains:

At some stage the wall had collapsed to what was then the contemporary ground level, and had had to be rebuilt with a new set of foundations. . . . As one looks at this wall face, one imagines that the whole of the lower wall will have vanished and the new stone foundations will run horizontally through the width of the wall. But in all the areas where the walls have been investigated, stages have occurred in which this was not so. For one reason or another, the face of at any rate the lower part of the wall alone has collapsed, leaving a cone-shaped core standing. The new wall, therefore, has been built in the shape of an inverted U, with two thin bases resting on new stone foundations on either face, and thickening as it rose over the diminishing core of the earlier wall. This gives the complication that if thereafter further erosion has taken place, the later wall easily disappears at the base, and appears at irregular heights depending on the local degree of erosion.

Some of the rebuilding was made necessary by the earthquakes that have always plagued Syria and Palestine. Periods of heavy rainfall must also have taken a toll in erosion, since these walls were of mud brick. And in at least one place, enemy action was responsible for the partial destruction of the wall. This was observed in Trench III, at the south end of the mound. Here the wall was exceptionally sturdy: fourteen feet thick, and still standing some ten feet high. Invaders kindled a fire so huge that a yard-deep layer of ash was found spreading out nearly twenty feet from the face of the wall. The intense heat burned the bricks red right to the center of the wall. The progress of the fire was aided by the presence of wooden beams that had been embedded in the wall to strengthen it; these caught fire and carried the heat inward. Though the wall itself did not collapse—the heat would have served to harden the bricks—the high temperatures fired the houses that adjoined the wall, and the blaze must have spread quickly through the town.

The patching and repatching of the outer walls went on steadily. Doubtless the city found itself in a state of virtually constant siege, since its location exposed it to the attack of nomads drifting into Palestine from the barren east. How the Early Bronze Age people of Jericho met these attacks we do not know, for the only weapons found in this level were a few copper daggers and a lone axhead. Their chief artillery may have been that of young David: stones hurled from slings. Such missiles would not proclaim their nature to the archeologists who found them fifty centuries later.

The fragmentary remains of the Early Bronze Age houses show them to be well-built and comfortable. The architects made extensive use of timber, particularly in their roofs. This probably contributed to Jericho's later problems, for, as the forests fell beneath Bronze Age axes, the hills of Palestine were laid open to erosion. Ignorant of conservationist ideas, the townsmen of Bronze Age Palestine destroyed their forests and turned their once-green land into a waste. By the time Solomon began to build his temple at Jerusalem in the tenth century B.C., he found it necessary to import timber from the Phoenician city of Tyre on the coast.

This period of rapid urban development and soil depletion may well have weakened the strength of Jericho so gravely that the city could no longer withstand the unending challenge of the nomads. About 2300 B.C., new invaders came and looked longingly at this wealthy, thriving metropolis, with its metal tools and its attractive pottery and its comfortable houses. The plump burghers of Jericho found themselves besieged, and in alarm they ordered the walls to be rebuilt once more.

It was a hurried job and a careless one. Crude stone foundations were laid atop the rubble of an earlier wall, and hasty brickwork was clapped into place. Many of the bricks were crumbling ones snatched from the ruins of other walls about the city. The wall was so poorly designed that it would surely have collapsed before it reached its full height, but that never had time to happen. The invaders set fire to the half-finished wall, building a towering pile of brush just as other invaders had done a few centuries earlier.

Thick deposits of ash mark the site; Kathleen Kenyon tells of "beautiful pastel shades of blues, greys, and pinks." The mud-colored brickwork was burned bright red clear through, and the furious heat swept through the loosely set masonry of the foundations and turned the city into a pyre. It was the end of Early Bronze Age Jericho. Right above the burned strata are found new types of pottery, thin and rough, and new styles of houses, haphazard and irregular. The invaders had taken possession.

Many tribes must have been afoot in those years. The evidence of the Jericho graveyard shows five separate and simultaneous types of burial, tagged by the archeologists as Square-shaft, Outsize, Dagger, Pottery, and Bead. Since each culture tends to maintain its own funeral customs without much variation, this indicates the probable presence of five independent tribal groups at Jericho at approximately the same time, each occupying its own section of the city.

The tribesmen held Jericho for about four centuries. It is likely that they belonged to the aggressive family of Semitic-speaking wanderers who were overrunning much of the Near East; during those same years, Semitic warriors overthrew the ancient Sumerian culture in Mesopotamia and caused chaos in Egypt. These simple desert folk constituted a sharp interruption of Bronze Age progress everywhere in the East, and for centuries thereafter their restless nature would bring confusion to the settled civilizations.

By 1900 b.c. stability began to return. Egypt had recovered from her time of troubles, and the strong rulers of the Twelfth Dynasty provided a steadying influence that radiated outward as far as Palestine and Syria. The semibarbarism of the nomads at Jericho yielded to returning civilization.

The squatters were driven off, it appears, by townsmen from the Syrian coast, who moved inland and took possession of the valley of the Jordan. Jericho, as always, was an attractive site for a town, and soon the great mound was growing higher as new builders added their contribution. This was the period now termed the Middle Bronze Age, marked by superb, delicate pottery, turned on a potter's wheel for the first time, and tools and weapons made entirely from the alloy bronze instead of from softer copper.

The houses of Middle Bronze Age Jericho, rising above layer upon layer of earlier dwellings, were close-set and solid. They show that life at Jericho must have been as comfortable then as in the palmiest days of the Early Bronze Age six hundred years before. Early in this period, the townsfolk protected their city with the customary brick wall, but later a new defensive system came into use, not only at Jericho but throughout Palestine. This was a steeply sloping bulwark of earth, faced by a thick, hard plaster layer and topped by a brick wall. The earth fill was itself an archeological treasure-trove, since the builders dumped whole refuse heaps into it, and it contained objects of all periods of Jericho's existence from the Neolithic onward.

Three of these earth-fill bulwarks were discovered. They were built at different times, perhaps as disturbances grew more frequent. The first, near the center of the mound, must have been formidable when intact: a stone foundation ten feet high, a plastered earth fill rising at an angle of 35 degrees to a height of more than thirty feet, and a steep brick wall about sixty feet high surmounting everything. The second bulwark has largely been destroyed; the third, which was the wall found by the German-Austrian expedition and ascribed to Joshua, survived as a massive stone foundation running three quarters of the distance around the mound.

These colossal fortifications were erected from about 1800 B.C. to 1600 B.C. Quite likely they were the work of the mysterious Hyksos, or "Shepherd Kings," the barbaric warriors who overran much of the ancient world at that time. They made themselves masters of Palestine and used it as the base for a successful invasion of Egypt in 1700 B.C. For the next century and a half Hyksos pharaohs ruled the land of the Nile, and in the cities of Palestine a Hyksos aristocracy could well have directed the construction of the unusual sloping fortifications that were characteristic of the period.

A tomb of Middle Bronze Age date at Jericho may have been the resting place of one of these warriors. Surrounding the body were the tokens of rank: a fine dagger, a battle-ax, a handsome bronze belt. Other weapons lay against the wall of the tomb. Offerings of pottery, notably a superb beaker molded in the form of a ram's head, indicated the dead man's importance. The skeletons of three horses or asses were discovered in the shaft of the vault, suggesting the likelihood that the success of the Hyksos was due to their unprecedented use of mounted cavalry.

Behind its vast walls, Jericho of the Middle Bronze Age thrived for centuries. But about 1580 B.C. came a stirring in Egypt, an uprising of the suppressed native aristocracy against the foreign overlords, and within a generation the Hyksos were driven out. The triumphant Eighteenth Dynasty of Egypt, not content to have expelled their former masters from their own boundaries, went on to penetrate Palestine and pursue the despised Hyksos far to the north. Under Pharaoh Thothmes I, Palestine and Syria became Egyptian as far as the Euphrates River.

The walled towns of Palestine must have felt the brunt of Thothmes' onslaught. Middle Bronze Age Jericho, with its winding streets and close-packed houses, had known centuries of peace, but destruction came swiftly. The graveyard shows signs of mass burials at this time, as though perhaps a plague had racked the city just before the invaders came. There could have been little resistance. Torches flamed in the streets, and Jericho died once more.

The destruction was thorough. Great jars were found in storage rooms, the grain in them blackened to carbonized crisps by the fire. Charred beams of second-story rooms lay everywhere, amid the fragments of pottery and other objects that had fallen when the timbers gave way. With such ruin visited on the city, the archeologists would not have been able to gather much of an impression of Middle Bronze Age artifacts—but for that always convenient habit of stocking tombs with the things of the world of the living.

From the cemetery at Jericho came a wealth of information about the city as it had been before it fell. Dozens of Middle Bronze Age tombs were found. The discovery of the cemetery itself, in 1952, was something of an accident. Arab refugees displaced by the partition of Palestine had been given the slopes north of Jericho as a camp. At first living in tents, the refugees had begun to build houses, and one of them, quarrying the soft limestone of the hills for mortar, came upon the shaft of a tomb. He brought an Egyptian scarab amulet to Miss Kenyon, who obtained permission from the refugees to conduct an excavation virtually in the streets of their settlement.

It developed that the refugee camp lay above an extensive cemetery whose tombs ranged in age from 3,000 to 5,500 years. The richest group belonged to the latter part of the Middle Bronze Age, roughly 1800–1560 B.C. These were vertical shafts that led to underground vaults. Apparently several generations of a family used the same vault, unceremoniously pushing the earlier burials to the rear of the chamber each time a new interment took place. As a result, only the final burial of each tomb was intact, with a jumble of bones and offerings in the background.

During her second season at Jericho, Miss Kenyon came upon six tombs of this period that had been sealed after simultaneous multiple burials, so that the offerings were undisturbed. The tombs cleared earlier had yielded pottery, scarabs, beads, a highly satisfactory harvest of archeological materials. These new tombs still contained, in addition, the highly perishable furnishings with which the dead had gone to their final repose. Wooden bowls, woven baskets, rush mats, beds, tables, combs, stools, platters, the remains of a wig, all were in incredibly fine states of preservation. Dishes contained dried steaks and joints, clusters of grapes, pomegranates, and vegetables.

The startled archeologists had not been prepared for such a cache of perfectly preserved objects. As they removed the boulders and clay that blocked the doorway of the first of these tombs, they peered in amazement through the gloom to see the bodies and offerings laid out neatly, as they had been left a millennium and a half ago.

By the uncertain light of a noisy portable generator they made their way into the tomb and began the painstaking process of clearing it. The opening of a tomb that has been sealed for thousands of years brings a special agony to the archeologist. The fragile objects begin to crack and splinter almost as soon as the moisture-laden outer air comes in contact with them. Immediate steps must be taken for their preservation. Yet the established practice of archeology demands that each object must be charted and photographed *in place* before it is handled or removed. The conflict is a tormenting one, for how can a cluttered tomb be properly recorded, a slow job at best, without allowing much of its contents to suffer?

When Charles Warren had excavated at Jericho in 1867, he found that, as he put it, objects "brought to the strong daylight vanished from view and returned into the dust from which they were constructed." This was a recurring lament in the writings of Layard and other pioneering archeologists, and frightful damage was done by these men before methods of preservation were developed.

At the beginning of the twentieth century, Flinders Petrie and others had used coatings of paraffin to protect perishable objects. It was a troublesome but effective way of staving off decay. The Kenyon team, however, making an attempt to be modern in all things, employed coatings of a plastic emulsion. They rapidly learned that the plastic did not sink into the material deeply enough to protect it. Telegrams flew back and forth, suggestions were offered, and in the end Miss Kenyon reverted to the old but still reliable method of using paraffin. A roaring primus stove joined the chugging generator in the tomb shaft, and the archeologists set about the job of preservation.

The finest tomb of all turned up at an awkward time, late in the afternoon as the day's work was about to halt. The excavators made the mistake of letting curiosity get the better of them; confronted with a sealed tomb, they could not resist rolling away the stone that covered its entrance, to get a quick peek. They were pleased and dismayed to find the tomb richer in wooden furniture than any of the others, which meant an emergency call had to go out for immediate work.

The toil continued till one in the morning—a photographer, a technical expert, and three other workers laboring at the tomb, whose entrance was 60 centimeters high and 50 centimeters wide. One archeologist crouched at the entrance, cleaning the objects within reach; with that cleared, a second archeologist stepped within, bent over since the chamber's roof was barely five feet high, having to remain motionless for fear of damaging something while he worked.

Each object had to be cleaned of dust before the paraffin could be applied. Then the wax was carefully dripped from a heated saucepan. "As one worked," Miss Kenyon wrote, "one could see the articles farther into the tomb starting to react to the outside air. A film of moisture would appear over the wood, whether condensation or exuding from the wood we are not quite sure, and one could see cracks appearing in front of one's eyes. There was a horrible sense of urgency, yet the delicacy of the work meant that one could not hurry."

The tomb contents afforded a detailed glimpse of the humbler goods of Middle Bronze Age Jericho households. The textiles, wooden furnishings, inlaid boxes, baskets, and mats gave a perspective far more comprehensive than potsherds and daggers could provide. Nowhere else in Palestine had so many perishable things of such great antiquity survived. Why these tombs should have protected their contents so superbly was a considerable puzzle to the archeologists. Professor F. E. Zeuner of the Institute of Archaeology of the University of London paid two visits to Jericho to study the unique tombs and concluded that subterranean gases, escaping from the valley floor, had penetrated the tombs and killed the bacteria of decay.

Whatever the reason, these unusual tombs permitted the archeologists to prepare an elaborate reconstruction of a room in a house of Middle Bronze Age Jericho. Every detail but for the costumes was wholly accurate: the bed, the tables, the stools, the mat, the baskets and boxes, even the platter of fruit on the table, derived entirely from the knowledge of the tombs.

Life was comfortable in the Jericho of 1600 B.C. But then came the onslaught. By the middle of the sixteenth century B.C., the site of Jericho was an abandoned ruin, and nearly two hundred years passed before it was again inhabited.

During that span of years, Eighteenth Dynasty Egypt rose to its magnificent zenith, then succumbed to internal confusions in the time of the heretic Pharaoh Akhnaten, whose monotheistic religious movement met with bitter resistance. The boy-pharaoh Tutankhamen had his brief reign and his glittering funeral; a general named Horemheb occupied the throne of Thebes for a generation; then the Nineteenth Dynasty came to power, and from 1304 B.C. onward the conquerors Rameses II and Rameses III led Egypt to renewed splendor. At some time during the thirteenth century B.C., the tribe of Israel, which had lived in bondage in Egypt for hundreds of years, set out across the wilderness of Sinai for Canaan, that land of milk and honey.

The Exodus of the Israelites may have taken place about 1260 B.C., in the reign of Rameses II. After long years of wandering, they came to the borders of the Promised Land and found the fortress city of Jericho before them. Once more the site beside Elisha's Fountain had been rebuilt. The Garstang expedition found Late Bronze Age tombs, which now are dated to about 1400 B.C., and the phantom remains of what must have been a small settlement built on the ruins of the Middle Bronze Age town. This was the occupation level of Jericho's rebirth, the beginning of the settlement that Joshua attacked.

The German-Austrian expedition had claimed in 1913 to have found the wall Joshua overthrew. Garstang showed in 1936 that that wall was much older than the Israelite conquest, and Kathleen Kenyon was able to identify it as Early Bronze Age, built at least a thousand years before Joshua's time. Garstang, in turn, had suggested that the sloping inner wall found by Sellin and Watzinger was Joshua's wall; but the Kenyon group showed it to be four centuries too old for that.

Where, then, was Joshua's Jericho?

Kathleen Kenyon could offer only an anticlimax: "Of the town walls of the Late Bronze Age, within which period the attack by the Israelites must fall by any dating, not a trace remains." Erosion had completely obliterated them. Of that Jericho, she could find nothing but a part of the kitchen of a single house and a single clay dipper that might have been dropped to the floor by a panicky housewife when the trumpets of the Israelites blared.

Nor was there a hint of the Jericho of Hiel the Bethelite, supposedly built in defiance of Joshua's curse almost five centuries later. That town too had been washed away by the centuries. On the uppermost levels of Tell es-Sultan, Miss Kenyon discovered some traces of Iron Age settlements of the seventh century B.C., and there the record halted. The next dwellers at Elisha's Fountain chose a different site to the west. The ancient mound was used only as a burial ground by the people of this Jericho of Roman times. When the Byzantine Greeks fell heir to Rome, they occupied Palestine and used Tell es-Sultan as a quarry for brick. A single stone house atop the mound marks this Byzantine period. In the seventh century A.D. came the invincible Arabs, and they have remained.

Kathleen Kenyon's excavation of Jericho was a textbook demonstration of modern archeological methods. With care and precision she and her co-workers laid bare a notable record of civilization extending back almost nine thousand years. They worked a revolution in historical thinking by demonstrating the unexpectedly advanced state of Neolithic culture at Jericho in the remote past.

The mound still remains. In its depths are hidden the secrets of the dawn of civilization. Future archeologists will return one day to cut through the heart of Tell es-Sultan and expose that first of all Jerichos, that oldest of mankind's settlements.

Two

Ugarit: A Cuneiform Alphabet

ON THE COAST of northern Syria, about twenty-five miles south of the Turkish frontier, is a bay called Minet-el-Beida, "White Harbor." The chalky cliffs that ring the harbor are brilliant in the Syrian sunlight, but at their seaward end they have crumbled, and the boulders in the sea are dangerous obstacles to shipping. Small boats can land on the sandy beach, and fishermen occasionally cast their nets there at night. Otherwise there are few visitors. The nearest sizable town, Latakia, is eight miles away.

Half a mile inland from the cove of Minet-el-Beida is a hillock some sixty-five feet high, known to the natives as Ras Shamra, or "Cape Fennel," from the fragrant plants that grow profusely on it. In the spring of 1928, a peasant plowing a field near this hillock struck a stone slab. He lifted it and found himself, like a character in the *Thousand and One Nights,* peering into an underground chamber.

A silt-choked passageway led him to a rectangular room that contained a cache of ancient objects, some of them of gold. These he extracted, and shortly they appeared on the antiquities market. Syria was then under French control as a League of Nations mandate. It was not long before the local governor, M. Schoeffler, heard of the discovery. After a visit to the spot, he notified the Department of Antiquities in Beirut. Soon French archeologists were arriving at Minet-el-Beida.

Charles Virolleaud, the Director of Antiquities, conducted brief and fruitless excavations. But some potsherds were found in the rubbish of the tomb the peasant had discovered, and these were sent to Paris for identification. René Dussaud of the Institut de

France studied them, reporting that they were similar to the pottery of the great civilization of Crete.* Professor Dussaud suggested that Minet-el-Beida had probably been a seaport in the second millennium B.C., visited by vessels of Crete, Cyprus, or the powerful Greek city of Mycenae, bringing ware of this type. Since Minet-el-Beida was well located on the Syrian mainland, just opposite the easternmost point of the island of Cyprus, it could easily have been an important stop in the trade route connecting the Mediterranean cultures with Egypt and Mesopotamia.

Further excavations seemed in order. The assignment went to Claude F. A. Schaeffer, a young French archeologist whose specialty up till then had been European prehistory. With seven camels carrying his luggage and equipment, Schaeffer arrived at Minet-el-Beida in March, 1929. A tent was pitched near the bay. In the morning, twenty Syrian soldiers arrived to protect the archeologist, since Turkish bandits had been roaming the neighborhood.

After looking the area over for a few days, Schaeffer hired some native workmen and began excavations on a slight rise about five hundred feet from the bay. The villagers, he wrote,

came timidly at first, because they believed I wanted to engage them as serfs; but when, after the first week, I paid every workman with good, hard silver, natives flocked in from far and near. News of the unexpected opportunity to earn money had spread with lightning speed. Also came idlers and thieves, who had an idea of making a little something on the side by stealing antiquities. . . . But they were discovered and sent away before they could do harm.

Exploratory trenches quickly turned up exciting finds. Working on an acre-wide area, Schaeffer dug parallel ditches and tallied eighty places of discovery. At depths of two to six feet he found handsome pottery of the Cretan and Cypriote style, large storage jars, a set of weights, and a well-preserved bronze figure of the Egyptian god Horus. Near this hawk-faced statuette was a smaller one, encrusted with gold, and a yard away lay the effigy of a seated god, Egyptian in style, his eyes encrusted with enamel

* See my *Lost Cities and Vanished Civilizations* (Chilton, 1962), pp. 63–92.

and silver. The international nature of the finds showed that this had indeed been a harbor where ships of many lands called.

A rider was dispatched to Latakia bearing a telegram for Paris. "The treasure of Minet-el-Beida is found!" Schaeffer exulted. He realized that he was uncovering an ancient graveyard and that the still-undiscovered ruins of the town must be nearby.

South of the main treasure-trove by about sixty feet Schaeffer came upon a flagstone-paved underground chamber, clearly an important tomb. It proved to be incomplete and empty, but its unusual design was a rewarding enough discovery. "In order that the dead kings should never go thirsty," Schaeffer wrote, a water-supply system had been built next to the tomb. Long stones with gutters chiseled in them led the water into the bottom of a large jar, from which the overflow ran off into the ground through holes pierced in a stone. In addition, for times of drought when springs ran dry, a walled-in well was built next to the water system. A window in the tomb was designed to enable the dead king to reach the well easily when thirsty.

Sixty-five feet to the west lay a second tomb, so large that it must certainly have been a royal resting place. Heavy flagstones covered the entry passage. As Schaeffer cleared the earth away, one of these precariously balanced flagstones tipped over, narrowly missing him and injuring a workman. It seemed that an earthquake had left the flagstones at an angle, and Schaeffer had unknowingly removed the earth that held them in place.

Cautiously, now, he cleared the passage, descending step by step toward the tomb. Painted vases and lamps were strewn over the steps. One of the lowest steps held an unbroken two-handled alabaster vase of Egyptian design. A step below it was a vase of Mycenaean style, and on the next step, before the entrance to the actual burial chamber, there lay the skull of a young man, perhaps the guardian of the tomb.

Only seven years earlier, Howard Carter and Lord Carnarvon had discovered the tomb of Tutankhamen—the most widely publicized and celebrated event in the history of archeology. As he studied the earthen wall of this Syrian burial chamber, Schaeffer could not help but wonder if some equally dazzling treasure awaited him here.

The workmen began to remove the earth that blocked the entrance. Soon came disappointment: a hole in the stone ceiling of the vault; one of Schaeffer's Syrians stuck his head through it from the outside and grinned at him. The tomb had been entered before. Plunderers had removed a keystone and slipped within. Tutankhamen's tomb, too, had been entered a short time after the young king's death, but the thieves had not been able to make off with much. Here, also, the hurried looters had seemingly taken only the most conspicuous objects of gold and silver, leaving a good deal for Schaeffer's delight.

Precious vases of glass, alabaster, and clay littered the floor; the thieves had crushed them underfoot as they moved about the tomb. In the dark corners of the chamber lay dishes, plates, and pitchers, and the skeletons of a man, a woman, and a child. In their haste, the intruders had overlooked gold beads and rings, an ivory casket, and other small treasures. The casket, probably a jewel box, was ornamented with an image of a seated goddess who closely resembled the fertility goddesses of Crete and Mycenae.

Summer was upon the excavators now. To avoid the heat, they worked from four to ten in the morning, then from three in the afternoon until late evening. Soon, though, it would be impossible to excavate at all. Schaeffer was eager to locate the city to which this cemetery belonged, so he temporarily suspended work in the necropolis and turned to the mound of Ras Shamra.

He hoped first to find the royal palace:

I decided to start my excavations on the highest point of the hill, where I had noticed a few traces of walls among the shrubs. The choice was fortunate. Below the upper layer of shapeless, weather-worn rocks hewn stones came to light. Somewhat deeper still we laid bare the foundation of a large building which must have been destroyed by fire, for ashes lay thick between the walls and blackened the hands of our workmen.

A bronze dagger and a bronze nail were unearthed, and then fragments of a life-size statue of an Egyptian pharaoh, with hieroglyphic-inscribed tablets nearby. Schaeffer uncovered a series of small rooms that reminded him of the storerooms of the sprawling palace at Knossos on Crete—and then, in a room divided by three pillars, he struck the find that gave the Ras Shamra excavation its archeological immortality: the royal library.

Libraries, not golden baubles, are the true treasures of archeology. The instances of such discoveries are few and monumentally important. The first was the library of the Assyrian king, Assurbanipal, discovered in 1853 in the ruins of Nineveh by Layard's assistant, Hormuzd Rassam. Later in the nineteenth century, American archeologists found the temple library of the ancient Sumerian city of Nippur, and Egyptian antiquity hunters produced the diplomatic archives of the monotheistic Pharaoh Akhnaten's capital at Tell el-Amarna. In 1906, Hugo Winckler found the archives of the Hittite kings at the Turkish city of Boghazköy. All these were hordes of clay tablets, most of them inscribed in the Sumerian or Akkadian languages of Mesopotamia. When translated, they presented an unsurpassable record of the history and culture of the Near East.

Schaeffer, examining in wonder his library of baked clay tablets atop the hill of Ras Shamra, saw that they, too, were in the cuneiform writing of Mesopotamia. He recognized inscriptions in Akkadian, the language of Babylonia and Assyria, which had been the international diplomatic language of the Near East 3,500 years ago. But many of the tablets, though written in the familiar wedge-shaped characters, did not look right. The cuneiform signs were not those of Akkadian or Sumerian. Nor were there enough different signs in the inscriptions. The various Mesopotamian cuneiform scripts were ideographic and pictographic in nature, with hundreds of signs, many of them standing for complex concepts or depicting in schematized form the actual appearance of the objects they represented. But the inscriptions on these tablets appeared to have hardly more than two dozen individual characters.

Schaeffer guessed that the Ras Shamra inscriptions were examples of some previously unknown cuneiform script that was phonetic in nature——that is, whose symbols stood for sounds rather than concepts. The earliest phonetic scripts were syllabaries, in which each character represented a specific consonant-vowel combination: *ba, be, bu, bo, bi,* and so on. The Cypriote and the Cretan Linear B scripts were of this sort. But syllabaries generally have fifty to a hundred characters. The amazed Schaeffer was forced to the conclusion that he had come upon a cuneiform script that was alphabetic in concept, each symbol standing for a single sound!

The oldest known alphabet, he knew, was the Canaanite or Phoenician one, a set of symbols devised some time after 2000 B.C. Its forgotten inventors probably based their ideas on the ancient picture writing of Egypt but abandoned the cumbersome ideographic system of the older civilization in favor of a flexible, easily handled set of twenty-odd phonetic characters. The merchants of the Levant no doubt found the alphabet handy in their business dealings, and its use spread throughout Syria, Palestine, and the Phoenician coast. The Greeks adopted and modified the Phoenician alphabet about 800 B.C., and the Romans made further modifications later, producing the letters we use today.

The alphabet's earliest history is still shrouded by time. Phoenician texts from Byblos of 1900 B.C. use a syllabic script with seventy characters, while three Canaanite inscriptions that may date from the eighteenth or seventeenth century B.C. employ ten different characters that appear to be forerunners of the later alphabetic ones. So the appearance of the alphabet can probably be dated to approximately 1800 B.C., although the evidence available so far is fragmentary.

Now, from Ras Shamra, had come something unexpected: an alphabet that used cuneiform characters and dated from the middle of the second millennium B.C. Since the ancient port at Ras Shamra's site had certainly been in contact with users of the Phoenician alphabet, it appeared as though this one city had borrowed the alphabetic concept but had chosen to adapt it to the ancient Mesopotamian method of writing on clay. The angular cuneiform characters were better suited for clay inscriptions than the symbols of the Phoenician script.

Schaeffer thought, in fact, that he had unearthed the oldest alphabet of mankind. It was a good four centuries older than the earliest Phoenician inscriptions known at that time; but within a few years, older Canaanite inscriptions were found that used ancestral forms of the well-known Phoenician alphabet. Whether or not the Ras Shamra alphabet was the world's first, it certainly was of great historical significance, and Schaeffer tenderly removed his precious clay tablets for study in Europe.

Before he ended his first season at Ras Shamra, he made another discovery in the same building: a pile of bronze tools and weapons, unusually well preserved. There were 4 large bronze swords, 11 lances, 27 axes, 14 hoes, and many other pieces. Some of these also bore inscriptions in the cuneiform alphabet.

It was June, and the temperature was unbearable. Schaeffer closed his shafts to protect them against treasure hunters and posted guards to watch over the hill until he could return the following spring. So that his fragile treasures would be spared the jouncing camel ride overland, he loaded them aboard a sailboat bound for Latakia. There they were carefully repacked, taken by car to Beirut, and shipped to France via diplomatic courier.

French scholars, headed by Charles Virolleaud, immediately tackled the problem of the Ras Shamra tablets. Virolleaud, as Director of Antiquities in Syria and Lebanon, was able to examine the tablets while they were still at Beirut. He could count only twenty-seven characters (scholars today distinguish thirty and sometimes thirty-two), and from that he drew the proper conclusion that the Ras Shamra script was alphabetic. But the Cypriote and Mycenaean pottery found at the site led him astray, and he hazarded a guess that the language of the inscriptions was Cypriote or possibly Mitannian, an Indo-European language spoken in a short-lived kingdom east of Syria.

Virolleaud published reproductions of some Ras Shamra tablets in the spring of 1930, along with his preliminary thoughts about their language. The cuneiform texts came to the attention of Hans Bauer, a German specialist in Oriental languages, who began an independent investigation.

Bauer was particularly an authority on Semitic languages, that family of tongues that includes Hebrew, Arabic, and such dead languages as Phoenician and Akkadian. A glance at the Ras Shamra inscriptions led him to think that they must be written in a Semitic language. On some tablets, the scribes had separated words with small vertical strokes, and that gave Bauer his foothold. He knew that in Semitic scripts—which leave the vowels unwritten—words could begin only with the letters *j, m, n,* and *t,* sometimes with *b, h, ḳ, l,* or *w,* and with the guttural sound *alef.* They could end only with the letters *h, ḳ, m, n, t, w,* or *j.* In many places Bauer found only a single letter between the word dividers, and these, assuming he was dealing with a Semitic language, could only be *l, m, b, ḳ,* or *w.*

It was a beginning. Bauer tabulated his possibilities and began to search for letter groupings that followed familiar Semitic structural rules. Soon it was clear that this still undecipherable script was broken into word patterns that were characteristically Semitic in order. Encouraged, Bauer used cryptographic methods to determine that one particular character was either an *m* or a *w,* and that another was either an *n* or a *t.* That was as far as he could go with his purely statistical tabulation. Now it was time to take a few judicious leaps toward conclusions.

Virolleaud had observed that a group of six characters engraved on the bronze axes was also found on one of the cuneiform tablets, preceded by another letter. He suggested that the six characters represented the name of the owner of the axes, and also the addressee of the tablets. The single preceding letter, then, might be a word meaning "to."

Bauer accepted the suggestion. In Hebrew and Phoenician, the single letter that means "to" is *l.* He assigned that value to the character. Searching the texts for words containing that character and either of the two that he had previously studied, Bauer found the *l* associated with the character he had identified as either an *m* or a *w,* followed by a third character. This word commonly appeared throughout the texts.

Could it be the Semitic word for "king?" That root was *m-l-ḳ,* the Hebrew *meleḳ,* Phoenician *milḳ.* Bauer accepted the first character as an *m* and temporarily called the still unknown third character *x.* Soon he found the grouping *m-l-x-x,* which corresponded to the Semitic *m-l-ḳ-ḳ,* "thy king." Now all three characters were deciphered—he hoped.

The deeper he got, the more correlations Bauer found. He located a one-letter word that had to be *b* and joined it to his *n*-or-*t* character as *b-n,* "son." The *b* also matched the *l* to form *b-l,* "Baal," the familiar Canaanite deity of the Old Testament.

"Baal" also yielded the Semitic explosive consonant *ayin*. When he found the *l* flanked by two identical consonants, Bauer could denote them as the symbols for *sh*, since the only Hebrew or Phoenician word consisting of *l* between two identical consonants is the numeral *sh-l-sh*, *"three."* And so the process went. In only a few weeks, Bauer declared that he had identified twenty Ras Shamra characters with certainty, and probably five more; only two rare ones eluded him.

Bauer's brilliant work was not quite perfect. He had made a few mistakes of attribution, and only seventeen of his suggested values were correct. The Ras Shamra language had been a Semitic dialect, related to but not identical with Hebrew. Bauer had drawn from the bronze axes the word for ax itself, *g-r-z-n* in written Hebrew; but actually the Ras Shamra word, it turned out later, had been *h-r-s-n*. His incorrect *g* and *z* led him to further errors.

His work was published in June, 1930. He explained his methods and conclusively proved the Semitic nature of the Ras Shamra language, illustrated by such god names as Baal, Asherah, and El, by the words for three and four, and by several other transliterations and translations.

The French scholars were impressed by Bauer's work. Men like Virolleaud and René Dussaud, who were closely involved with the Ras Shamra project, accepted Bauer's findings as fundamentally correct, though recognizing that errors were present. When Bauer's articles reached the French Biblical and Archaeological School at Jerusalem, they came to the attention of Édouard Dhorme, an archeologist who had served as a cryptographer in World War I, and Dhorme detected the places where Bauer had gone astray. He communicated these to Bauer. By October, 1930, Bauer published an expanded version of his earlier articles under the title *The Decipherment of the Cuneiform Tablet of Ras Shamra*. It incorporated Dhorme's corrections, and now twenty-five of the cuneiform signs were accurately established. Rarely has an unknown ancient script been cracked so swiftly.

By this time, Claude Schaeffer and another archeologist named Georges Chenet had completed a second season of work at Ras Shamra. They uncovered more tombs at the bay of Minet-el-

Beida, and, working high on the Ras Shamra mound, they entered the ruins of an immense thick-walled temple, whose courtyard contained broken statues of the Egyptian Eighteenth Dynasty style. South of this temple was the building that had housed the collection of tablets. Schaeffer had erroneously thought that this was the royal palace, but now he realized that it was the dwelling of a high priest associated with the adjoining temple. The cache of bronze tools and weapons found in the building had been temple offerings, donated to the high priest and inscribed to him by the smith who had fashioned them. The collection of tablets had been the temple library.

A school for scribes had been part of this building complex, it appeared. The archeologists found many more large tablets covered with cuneiform texts, some of them dictionaries in several languages. One column of a dictionary tablet used the Ras Shamra alphabet, the next gave the Babylonian equivalents, and the third column listed the corresponding words in the old Sumerian tongue, which even then was a dead language used only by scholars and lawyers, as Latin is in modern times. One tablet amusingly illustrated the inexperience of its scribe; he had carelessly written across the border of his column, so that it was necesary for him to trace a ragged line separating the trespassing left-hand column from the right-hand one, and, running out of space toward the end of his tablet, he had had to reduce the size of his characters to the point of illegibility.

The first year's texts from Ras Shamra had chiefly been incomplete lists and inventories; the new finds were extensive documents, perhaps narrative poems or works of history. They were hurried to Paris, where Virolleaud set to work on them at once. Armed with his knowledge of the Ras Shamra alphabet, he could report that the texts were of the highest importance: letters, religious rituals, a long epic poem, commercial documents, and much else that cast light on the ancient Near East.

The identity of the ruined city at the Ras Shamra mound no longer was a mystery. It was identified now as Ugarit, a prosperous port frequently mentioned in the Tell el-Amarna letters, the Hittite archives of Boghazköy, and other records found in earlier document caches. Ugarit, with its highly favorable location, had played a central role in the delicate politics of the Near East thirty-five centuries ago. It lay at the crossroads of several trade routes linking Egypt and Mesopotamia with Canaan, Asia Minor, Crete, Cyprus, and the Aegean world. Easily reached from Egypt by sea and from the Hittite homeland in Asia Minor by land, Ugarit of necessity had to tread cautiously in the rivalry between these two powerful kingdoms. The annals of many nations showed that the wily merchants of Ugarit were able to steer a course nimbly between the contending powers, taking their profits where they could, submerging their own local pride for the sake of safety and prosperity.

Our knowledge of Ugarit is twofold. Claude Schaeffer provided the archeological record, the testimony of the spade, showing the ebb and flow of Ugaritic life as depicted by the artifacts in the mound. Schaeffer dug at Ras Shamra from 1929 to 1939 and returned in 1950 for several further campaigns. His careful stratigraphic work won him high praise from his colleagues.

At the same time, the Ras Shamra tablets, found by Schaeffer and deciphered by Bauer, Virolleaud, and Dhorme, yielded a unique fund of information about Ugaritic religion, history, and customs. Kathleen Kenyon's work at Jericho had to be conducted in the absence of any documentary evidence whatever, except for the Biblical passages; but the unearthing of Ugarit benefited from the extra dimension provided by the texts. From the library of the Ugaritic king Niqmadd, found by Schaeffer in 1929 and still not fully plumbed, has come not only new light on the evolution of the alphabetic concept but also material of the highest value in reconstructing the development of Hebrew religious thought.

Schaeffer's excavations showed that the Minet-el-Beida region had been inhabited by man from his first appearance in Syria. A few miles north of Ras Shamra, primitive stone axes many thousands of years old were discovered on the bank of a stream. The occupation of Ras Shamra itself began somewhat later, perhaps about the time that Jericho was founded. Driving his trench right through Ras Shamra until he came to the rocky surface of the original hill, some fifty-five feet down, Schaeffer found traces of the Neolithic settlement there. Flint and bone tools were scattered about. This layer may be eight to ten thousand years old, but the Neolithic dwellers at Ras Shamra were not as advanced as those of Jericho at that time.

The layers just above yielded shards of reasonably capable pottery, six or seven thousand years old. The resemblance of this pottery to the ware of other Syrian and Palestinian cities shows that widespread commerce was likely to have existed in the area. In the next level, about six feet from the bottom, Schaeffer found evidence of Copper Age development and highly accomplished pottery. A few feet higher up were the deposits of five thousand years ago. These contained pottery of a Mesopotamian style, indicating probable contact between Ugarit and the prosperous cities of Sumer. The Sumerians, dwelling in an alluvial plain, had no building materials available other than mud, and doubtless imported timber and stone from the cities of the Syrian coast—including Ugarit.

About 2400 B.C., the Semitic-speaking Sargon of Akkad conquered the cities of Sumer and founded a powerful though ephemeral empire in Mesopotamia. An inscription of Sargon's claims the conquest of "the land of the sunset and the mountains of cedar, all of it," which implies that he visited the cities of Syria and perhaps Ugarit. Sargon's empire fell in a century's time, overrun by barbarians out of Persia, and the entire East suffered economic dislocations. The mound at Ras Shamra reflects this, for its strata of this period yielded crude pottery and other indications of impoverishment.

During this time of stress, Semitic tribes were on the march. We have already seen how nomads put an end to Early Bronze Age Jericho about 2300 B.C., ushering in four centuries of chaos. But by 1900 B.C., order had been restored at Jericho and throughout all the land that we know as Canaan. Ugarit, at the opposite end of Canaan from Jericho, also returned to prosperity.

The exact whereabouts of Canaan deserves clarification here. The word itself derives from Kinahna, by which name the Babylonians called the Syrian coast from the Gulf of Alexandretta to Carmel Head. From that strip of coast came *kinahhu,* the coveted purple dye made from native shellfish. But gradually Canaan came to include all of Syria, taking in that part of the coast now called Lebanon. When the Israelites invaded Palestine in the thirteenth century B.C., they applied the term "Canaanites" loosely to all the prior inhabitants of Palestine as well as Syria. From this Old Testament usage, we group all the pre-Israelite cultures of Syria, Lebanon, and Palestine as Canaanite. After the Hebrew conquest, Canaan was divided between the Phoenicians of the coast and the Israelites inland and to the south.

Mesopotamia, about 1800 B.C., was enjoying a vigorous revival under the Babylonian dynasty founded by the great lawgiver Hammurabi. Ugarit seems to have had extensive trade with Babylonia, becoming one of the chief ports for the export of Mesopotamian goods to the Mediterranean cultures. It was during this epoch that the great temples, palaces, and tombs found by Schaeffer were first constructed, and probably about this time that the alphabetic script appeared. A rich poetic literature was set down on clay tablets.

Instability came again to the Near East about 1700 B.C. Egypt fell victim to the Hyksos, Babylonia to invaders called the Kassites. A new power arose in Asia Minor, the warlike Hittites, who dared to attack and plunder the mighty city of Babylon itself about 1595 B.C. Another new state, the Indo-European kingdom of Mitanni, took form shortly after. One army after another rampaged through Canaan, the pathway for conquest.

Ugarit, contemplating the possibility of invasion from Mitanni or the Hittites, needed a protector. Mesopotamia was far away, and the Babylonians had fallen upon evil times; besides, the land of Mitanni now interfered with contact between Syria and Mesopotamia. The only trustworthy power to which Ugarit could turn was Egypt.

Egypt had been Ugarit's ally at an earlier time of troubles, about 2000 B.C. With the East in chaos, Ugarit had negotiated a treaty of friendship with the powerful pharaohs of the Twelfth Dynasty. Schaeffer found gifts of amulets and carnelian beads sent to Ugarit by Senusret I, and a statue of Khnumit, the wife of Senusret II—perhaps a princess of Ugarit who had been sent to Egypt as pharaoh's bride. Pharaoh Amenemhet III had donated two inscribed sphinxes to stand at the entrance to the Temple of Baal. But the Hyksos conquest of Egypt interrupted this pact. The Hyksos took control of the Canaanite cities, as well, and multilated the sphinxes and statuettes erected by the pharaohs at Ugarit.

After the expulsion of the Hyksos about 1555 B.C., Egypt's Eighteenth Dynasty sought to re-establish the sphere of influence created by the Twelfth. Ugarit willingly submitted to Egyptian power. The three warrior pharaohs named Thothmes led victorious armies through Syria and used Ugarit, the best port on the coast, as a staging point. In the reign of the bloody Amenhotep II, who came to the Egyptian throne in 1448 B.C., an Egyptian garrison was stationed at Ugarit.

But a cosmopolitan port such as Ugarit maintained ties with all possible markets. The wealthy Minoan culture of Crete sent merchant ships regularly to Ugarit, and the Cretans maintained permanent offices there. Cypriote merchants and those of the powerful Aegean cities also settled at Ugarit. Some Mitannians resided there, and also Hurrians, the submerged original people of Mitanni. With this mixed background, it is easy to see why the school for scribes at Ugarit maintained a voluminous collection of multilingual dictionaries.

The Hurrians and Mitannians attained considerable influence in Ugarit; Niqmadd, Ugarit's king at the time the great library was assembled, had a Hurrian-sounding name. These outsiders tried to deflect Ugarit away from collaboration with Egypt and toward an alliance with Mitanni. In the middle of the fifteenth century B.C., while Amenhotep II was waging war in Mitanni, his garrison at Ugarit was suddenly confronted with a local uprising. The pharaoh returned hurriedly to quell it. By 1440 B.C., Egypt and Mitanni had concluded an alliance themselves, aimed at the Hittites, and Ugarit flourished in this time of tranquility. Even after the Hittites had destroyed the Mitannian kingdom about 1380 B.C., Ugarit remained in peace, thanks to its shrewd policy of bending with prevailing currents.

The Hittites, when they had finished with Mitanni, moved on into Syria. In theory all of Syria and Palestine owed tribute to Egypt; but now the unworldly Akhnaten was on the Egyptian throne, and in his preoccupation with religious reformation he took no steps to safeguard Egypt's interests in the north. The Tell el-Amarna letters, the diplomatic archives found at Akhnaten's ruined capital, offer a melancholy record of Hittite encroachment in Syria. One Syrian prince after another begged Akhnaten to send troops; and the pharaoh made no reply. The Hittites used puppet Syrian rulers to conquer city after city.

Ugarit, closest of all the Syrian ports to Hittite territory, found it advisable to pay tribute to the Hittites. A letter to Akhnaten from the Ugaritic king tactfully described the necessity for this. Soon, Ugarit was actively aiding the Hittites, as it became apparent that Akhnaten would not stir to resist the loss of his Syrian tributaries. Ribaddi of Byblos, a prince loyal to Egypt, lamented, "I can no longer send my ships to get wood from Ugarit. . . . The land is no longer safe." A later letter from Ribaddi informed Akhnaten that Ugarit and all the lands around it had gone over to the enemy.

Then came what may have seemed like retribution: an earthquake and a tidal wave struck Ugarit. Another loyalist, Abimilki of Tyre, wrote to Akhnaten to declare, "Ugarit, the king's town, has been destroyed by fire; half the town has been burnt, the other half is no more." The port quarter was devastated. Claude Schaeffer uncovered ruined houses, the walls still leaning and cracked. But the city was rebuilt.

The long-delayed frontal collision between Egypt and the Hittites took place about fifty years later, during the reign of Rameses II. Two huge armies met at the Syrian town of Kadesh in 1290 B.C., and the ensuing battle was so ambiguous in its results that both sides claimed victory. The Egyptian secret service noticed a contingent of Ugaritic forces fighting on the Hittite side at Kadesh. But the battle, though it did not end Hittite control over Syria, was the first serious failure the Hittites had suffered in a hundred years. Ugarit, sensing a shift in the breeze, began to side with Egypt again, though continuing to pay tribute to the Hittites.

When Rameses II and the Hittite king Hattusilis III signed a treaty of peace in 1269, Ugarit reaped the reward of its shrewdness. It had survived the three-way jockeying among Egypt, Mitanni, and the Hittites and prospered now once more, doing business with all comers. The city reached its peak of expansion.

The big tombs with their ingenious libation channels were built at this time. Schaeffer, discovering the first two, had thought they were royal tombs, but by 1939 he had found twelve more, all of contemporary age, and he realized that they were the sepulchers of wealthy Ugaritic families. Examination of the skeletal remains led him to conclude that these Ugaritic plutocrats were not of the basic Semitic stock of Canaan but rather were of Aegean ancestry, perhaps Mycenaeans. He suggested that "the Aegean-Mycenaean and Cypriotic colony at Ugarit, so important from the beginning of the fifteenth century [B.C.], was augmented by numerous immigrants. We may compare them with the Greeks and Armenians who today throng the ports of the Levant and monopolize business to the detriment of the less enterprising natives."

Soon, however, more Mycenaeans arrived at Ugarit: not settlers but refugees. Barbarians known only as the "Sea People" descended on the Mediterranean world and laid waste to the great cities of the Aegean civilization. Fires blazed in the cities of Agamemnon and Menelaus. Minoan Crete had already been overwhelmed, perhaps by these Sea People, perhaps by the Mycenaeans. Having shattered the Mycenaean world, the invaders turned eastward. They devastated the land of the Hittites so thoroughly and so rapidly that not a word of the conquest was recorded in the Hittite archives. Leaving Asia Minor smoldering, these unstoppable conquerors struck at Syria by land and by sea. About 1150 B.C. they passed through Ugarit, leaving a dead city behind. Some of its people sought refuge on the neighboring island of Cyprus, where settlements of the twelfth century B.C. reveal Ugaritic motifs.

Ugarit was forgotten by time. The harbor that had been the source of its prosperity became blocked by sand and gravel thrown up by the stormy seas of winter, and by soil and rubble carried down from the inland hills by swollen streams. The shoreline altered, so that what once had been a port now lay half a mile inland. About 600 B.C., a small settlement existed atop the mound that had been Ugarit, and Greek ships called there in the following century. But gradually the last few occupants of the hill abandoned it. The Arab peasants who lived nearby gave it the name of Ras Shamra and pastured their sheep on the site of the necropolis of Ugarit. And the city beneath the mound slept undisturbed until 1928.

The tombs and temples and palaces of Ugarit are of notable archeological interest, particularly the sumptuous royal dwelling discovered by Schaeffer in his early seasons at Ras Shamra and more completely excavated by him in the 1950's. When he halted work in 1953, Schaeffer had laid bare sixty-seven rooms of this palace, sprawling over more than twelve thousand square yards, and much still remained buried. There were five courtyards, eleven great staircases, seven porticoed entrances. The rooms reserved for royal scribes produced a fresh harvest of tablets in 1953, dealing with political, diplomatic, and economic matters. They included letters to the Hittite and Egyptian monarchs, treaties of alliance, the records of subtle negotiations—what Schaeffer refers to as history "written by the very actors of the great contest of the fourteenth and thirteenth centuries."

Indeed, the tablets of Ugarit are the most significant finds of Ras Shamra. They comprise a vast, virtually unequaled documentation of Canaanite life: tax lists, real estate transactions, letters of credit for dealings in commodities such as wine, oil, vinegar, copper, and lead, a manual for veterinary surgeons, royal decrees, the will of a king, the inventory of the trousseau of a queen whose gold jewelry alone weighed thirty-three pounds, and much else. Nothing like this has come down to us from other Canaanite cities, since only at Ugarit did scribes write on durable tablets of clay; the papyrus records of the contemporary towns long since have rotted in the wet climate of the Syrian coast. The unique alphabet of Ugarit was probably an adaptation of Canaanite concepts to Mesopotamian techniques, and only through that happy joining did such a generous proportion of Ugaritic culture survive.

The religious texts of Ras Shamra are the most significant, for they have afforded a total reinterpretation of Canaanite religion. Not until the decipherment of the Ugaritic tablets was it realized what a powerful element of Canaanite theology is present in the religion of the patriarchs of Israel.

The Canaanites emerge from the pages of the Old Testament

with what would today be called a poor image. The Israelite authors of the scriptural books, proud of their own lofty monotheism, depicted the Canaanites as depraved idolaters, abhorrent heathens, whose ways were to be abjured. "After the doings of the land of Canaan, whither I bring you, shall ye not do," the Lord declared to Moses. "Defile not ye yourselves in any of these things: for in all these the nations are defiled which I cast out before you: And the land is defiled: therefore I do visit the iniquity thereof upon it, and the land itself vomiteth out her inhabitants."

The abominations of the Canaanites brought down the wrath of the Almighty, and their lands were given over to the Israelites. Thereafter it remained to Israel a constant temptation to slide back into the ways of these monstrous blasphemers: "The children of Israel did evil in the sight of the Lord, and forgat the Lord their God, and served Baalim and the groves." Prophets such as Hosea thundered against the infiltration of Canaanite customs among his people: "They [the Israelites] sacrifice upon the tops of the mountains, and burn incense upon the hills, under oaks and poplars and elms, because the shadow thereof is good. . . . For Israel slideth back as a backsliding heifer."

The great revelation of the Ras Shamra texts was that these abominable Canaanites were not so abominable after all. They worshiped many gods, which by our standards makes their religion less advanced than that of the Israelites. But their iniquities and blasphemies seem to be nothing more dreadful than a nature cult of the sort that the Israelites themselves probably had before their monotheistic ideas evolved. The fierce terms that the Old Testament prophets hurl at the Canaanites represent, it seems, the hostility that an evolving culture nearly always feels for the culture level it has just left behind.

Since Judaism, like all living religions, is jealous of its origins, it is a controversial matter to contradict the established scriptures. The Old Testament portrays the Israelites as the Chosen of God from earliest times, their austere monotheistic creed standing out in sharp relief against the idolatry all about it. A more objective view holds that, until about 2000 B.C., the Hebrews were simply one of the many nomadic desert tribes of the Near East, speaking a Semitic tongue and worshiping a variety of gods and demons known collectively as the *elohim*. These were deities of nature, inhabiting rocks and trees and streams, bringing heat and thirst, rain, sandstorms. During the widespread movement of Semitic tribes about 2000 B.C., a leader whom we know as Abraham brought the Hebrews out of Mesopotamia and westward into northern Syria, then downward into Palestine. Here they mingled with related tribes, the Canaanites. We have no reason to suspect that their religion was greatly different from that of the Canaanites.

At some point the Hebrews began to prefer one of the *elohim* above all others. This *el,* this god, may have been called El-Shaddai, "the El of the Mountains." They continued, though, to pay homage to the other gods of their cycle of fertility myths. Then came a lengthy sojourn in Egypt, lasting until about 1260 B.C. When the Hebrews emerged under the leadership of Moses, they had been introduced to a new god, Yahweh, a tempestuous volcano-spirit, stern and vindictive, quite different from the benevolent agricultural deity El-Shaddai.

Now they returned to Canaan after an absence of five or six centuries. The Canaanites, cousins to the Hebrews, still worshiped their many *elohim*. But the Hebrews now clung to the standard of Yahweh. And a new element had entered, for they insisted that Yahweh was the *only* god. It may be that they had acquired this monotheistic idea from Akhnaten, the revolutionary pharaoh who ruled Egypt from 1377 to 1361 B.C., but this is only a speculative suggestion.

What does not appear speculative is the argument that the Hebrews worshiped the many *elohim* of Canaan before they became monotheists. The plural word *elohim* survived all editing and remained in the Old Testament as one of the Hebrew names for God—a fossilized outcropping, so to speak, of the earlier belief. And the fury of the Yahweh-worshiping Israelites against those who would backslide to the Canaanite religion of El and Baal has the sound of an attempt to break with a disreputable past and to hide any indebtedness to it.

Until the Ras Shamra tablets were translated, though, the religion of Canaan was known to us only as portrayed by the Hebrews—which is to say, as a nest of abominations. As Claude Schaeffer observed:

The tone of moral indignation which pervades the judgment of the Israelites is obviously tinged by the desire to injure their adversary at all costs. With the same interests at stake these accusations are as biased as were the criticisms levelled at the pagan world by certain Christian historians. As it is, the Ras Shamra texts reveal a literature of a high moral tone, tempered with order and justice.

The Canaanites were farmers, and their gods were gods of the field. At the head of the pantheon is El, termed "the Father of Men," "the Creator of Created Things." He is the supreme judge who reigns over all. "No one can change that which El hath fixed," one of the texts declares. He is the great father, the counterpart of the Greek Zeus, the Roman Jupiter, the Norse Odin. He is often represented as a mighty bull, which found its echoes in the Greek myths of Zeus's escapades in that form.

El and his consort Asherah, or Asherat, the mother-goddess, dwell somewhere in the west, where the rivers flow into the sea. They are kindly but remote figures, ruling from afar and rarely meddling in the activities of men. The deity closest to mankind is Baal, the son of El. He is not the foul demon depicted by the Biblical prophets but rather a vigorous and well-loved hero who brings fertility to the fields.

The texts call Baal "the Mighty," "Mightiest of Heroes," "the Prince." He rules over storm, wind, and rain. His voice is heard when thunder booms; lightning flashes from Baal's hand; he is young and active, endowed with irrepressible vitality. Baal is associated with two fertility-goddesses whose functions overlap somewhat: the ferocious warrior-maiden Anat, his sister, and the beautiful Astarte, known to the Babylonians as Ishtar and undoubtedly the model for the Aphrodite of the Greeks.

Baal's nemesis is Mot, the summer-god who brings heat and drought. The struggle between Baal and Mot, spring and summer, rain and heat, is a central theme of the mythological texts of Ugarit. Sometimes Mot is shown contending with Aliyan, Baal's son, the god of springs and underground waters, but the essential conflict is the same.

These are the chief figures of the Canaanite pantheon. There are many others: Dagon, a corn-god; Reshef, who can be roughly equated to Apollo; Kothar, a sea-god; and Hijon, the goldsmith (Vulcan, Hephaestos) of the gods. But the texts concerned with these deities are fragmentary, and the dozens of subsidiary Canaanite gods are not well known to us.

The epic poems that deal with the life of Baal give us the myths that underlie Canaanite religious thinking. Probably these myth cycles were recited regularly at the shrines of the gods. The gods were worshiped at springs and wells and particularly on hilltops, the notorious "high places" so ringingly condemned by the Biblical prophets. Offerings of sheep and cattle were presented, and the sacrifices were divided among the worshipers after the vital organs had been burnt in honor of the gods.

The religion had an immediate and direct function: to insure the growth of the crops and the generosity of the harvest. At the religious festivals, the phases of the agricultural year were translated into symbolic terms, and these became the material of myth.

The great poem of Baal, unearthed between 1929 and 1933, is hundreds of lines long. It tells how Baal won kingship over land and sea, while his father El looked on benignly, encouraging his son's battles without interfering in them. A lengthy passage describes the building of the "house of Baal," which corresponds in its physical details to the temple of Baal excavated by Schaeffer at Ras Shamra. Apparently of all the gods only Baal had no house, an injustice which El remedies at the insistence of Baal's sister Anat. El gives the word that all the subsidiary gods are to take part in the work. When he is properly housed, Baal can serve his function as a bringer of rain:

> Moreover Baal will send abundance of his rain,
> Abundance of moisture with snow,
> And he will send forth his voice in the clouds,
> His flashing to the earth in lightning.

The house of Baal is finally built after some further disputes among the gods. The sea-god Kothar volunteers to make a window or skylight in the temple, but Baal forbids it. Kothar grows angry, spits his defiance, cries, "Thou'lt heed my words, O Baal!" When the house is finished, Baal decides that he needs a window after all, as the opening through which rain can fall upon the earth. Kothar laughs and says in effect, "I told you so, Baal!" The window is made and thunder sounds as Kothar opens it, letting rain descend from the clouds.

A housewarming feast follows, and the gods disperse. A gap in the text makes unclear the relevance of an ensuing passage in which Baal's sister Anat runs amok, "'Smiting the Westland's people, smashing the folk of the Sunrise." This graphic but puzzling section shows Anat wading through heaps of severed heads and hands:

> She plunges knee-deep in knights' blood,
> Hip-deep in the gore of heroes. . . .
> Her liver swells with laughter,
> Her heart fills up with joy.

Baal, at the height of his supremacy, looks now toward his enemy, Mot, his rival for the kingship over gods and men. He sends two messengers to Mot's underworld home, bearing a defiant decree. Mot's response is uncertain, because the text again is fragmentary, but it is enough to make Baal himself go to the underworld to deal with Mot. Next comes a mournful announcement from messengers arriving at El's court:

> We came upon Baal, fallen on the ground:
> Great Baal is dead, the Prince, Lord of Earth, is perished.

Spring has been slain by summer's baleful heat—an event celebrated in many mythologies. El gashes his cheeks in mourning, pours ashes on his head. A weeping Anat wanders dismally in search of her brother, just as Isis seeks Osiris in Egyptian myth, Ishtar looks for Tammuz in Mesopotamian stories, Aphrodite for Adonis in the Greek. She finds Baal and buries him. The world is plunged into sadness. A new king is needed for the gods, and Ashtar, a sky-god, is nominated. He climbs upon Baal's throne, "But his feet reach not down to the footstool, nor his head reaches up to the top."

The parched earth is blistered by Mot's heat. The summer-god reigns, now, and how will next year's crops grow if Baal is not alive to bring them rain? The bereaved Anat seeks out Mot and grabs the hem of his robe.

> She lifts up her voice and cries:
> Now, Mot! Deliver my brother.

Mot refuses, sneeringly describing how he ripped Baal apart with his teeth. He will not restore the god to life. Anat, whose fierceness has already been unforgettably portrayed, loses her temper:

> She seizes Mot the son of El,
> With a sword she cleaves him,
> With a flail she threshes him,
> With a fire she doth burn him,
> With a millstone she grinds him;
> In a field she scatters him;
> The birds eat his remains, the wild creatures
> consume his fragments.

This is obviously a symbolic representation of the harvest, the climax of the summer growing season. Though Anat has threshed Mot and ground him, he does not disappear from the story. Summer is over. Winter, the time of Baal, is approaching. Aliyan, Baal's son, contends with Mot, and then miraculously Baal himself is alive once more, hurling his thunderbolts and booming his thunderous defiance at Mot. The two gods meet in direct combat:

> They glare at each other like glowing coals;
> Mot is strong, Baal is strong;
> They thrust at each other like wild oxen;
> Mot is strong, Baal is strong;
> They bite like serpents;
> Mot is strong, Baal is strong;
> They kick like stallions;
> Mot is down, Baal is down on top of him.

Baal triumphs. The rains and snows of winter come, and then the green spring. But the cycle is eternal, and Mot will force Baal into submission the following summer, only to meet defeat once again after the harvest.

[51]

These dramatic myths lack the high moral fervor of the Old Testament stories, there is nothing in this brawling of seasonal gods to match in power the episode of Abraham's intended sacrifice of Isaac, for example. To that extent the Israelites had reason to feel disdain for the Canaanite religion. But it was out of that simple, unsophisticated peasant cult that their own beliefs evolved, and there is more than a little concern with ethical matters in the Ras Shamra texts. With their urgent expression of faith that order will triumph over chaos, their preoccupation with justice and equity, the Canaanite texts show depths of feeling that scarcely merit the bitter denunciations of the Old Testament.

Though the Israelites rejected the Canaanite religion in favor of a more elevated theology, their scriptures show that they did not escape altogether from the Canaanite background they were so eager to conceal. The presence of references to Elohim in the Old Testament is one clue. In 1936, a Biblical scholar named H. L. Ginsberg published the first of a series of studies that demonstrated in detail the debt of Hebrew literature to the Canaanites.

Examining the newly translated tablets of Ras Shamra, Ginsberg found that a characteristic form of Hebrew verse was commonly found in the older Ugaritic texts, and that there were parallels both in structure and in content. A passage from the Baal epic relating the battle between Baal and the dragon Yam reads this way:

> Behold, thine enemies, O Baal,
>> Behold, thine enemies shalt thou crush,
>> Behold, thou shalt smite thy foes!

A similar passage is found in the 92nd Psalm:

> For behold, Thine enemies, O Lord,
>> For behold, Thine enemies shall perish,
>> All doers of evil shall be scattered!

Other stylistic relationships could be cited to show that the Hebrew poets were thoroughly familiar with the epics of Canaan. The sea-monster Leviathan of Isaiah is the Lotan of the Baal epic, and the same adjectives are used to describe him: "that piercing serpent," "that crooked serpent." The new knowledge gathered at Ras Shamra has even helped to clarify some puzzling problems of the Bible's Hebrew text. The Hebrew word *beth-heber,* translated "wide house" in the King James version, had to be reinterpreted after its Ugaritic equivalent, *bit-khuburi,* came to light. In its cuneiform context, the word meant "brewery" or "beerhouse," and the previously mysterious Biblical phrase became more clear when the translation read, "It is better to live in the corner of a roof-terrace than with a brawling woman in a beerhouse."

Claude Schaeffer's excavation of Ugarit was a landmark of modern archeology. It spawned a scholarly discipline, Ugaritic studies, that did not exist before the Ras Shamra tablets were found. Few archeological endeavors have produced so much information about an entire culture from a single site. Though the mound of Ras Shamra has not yet given up all its riches, it has already had a dynamic impact on every aspect of our knowledge of the ancient Near East.

Three

A CHINESE STUDENT who attended school in the nineteenth century had almost five thousand years of his
country's history to master. The record of dynasties,
invasions, great philosophers, and political shifts was burdened
with a weight of names and dates of enormous proportions,
stretching back into the mists of antiquity.

The convenient division of Chinese history into dynastic periods made things a little easier for the embattled schoolboy. There
was the currently reigning dynasty, first of all, the Ch'ing or
Manchu, which had been supreme in China since 1644. Before
that came the Ming, when art flourished but emperors were
hopelessly corrupt; still earlier, the Yüan or Mongol Dynasty of
Kublai Khan, the Sung of glorious porcelains, and the gaudy
T'ang and potent Han, and so on back to the Ch'in Dynasty,
whose tyrannical founder built the Great Wall of China between
221 and 214 B.C.

All this was documented by a wealth of historical records. So,
too, was the Chou Dynasty that had preceded the Ch'in. The
oldest Chinese records dated from the Chou period and carried
the flow of history back without break to the Chinese equivalent
of 841 B.C.

But China's civilization had already been ancient then, the
schoolboy of seventy or eighty years ago was taught. Of course,
there were no authentic documents that actually survived from
the time before the Chou. But there were many works of history
that claimed to be Chou or Han copies of much older writings,
and who could deny that they were? No doubt the originals had

been lost centuries ago, but the traditional-minded Chinese were willing to accept the latter-day copies as genuine.

And so it was possible to push Chinese history back beyond 841 B.C., although there was some disagreement about the chronology. The Chou Dynasty, it was taught, had seized power in 1027 B.C. (though one system of dating put it at 1122 B.C. and another at 1050). Out of the western marches had come the Chou to overthrow a predecessor dynasty, the Shang, who had ruled since 1523 B.C. (or 1765, or 1558). The Shang aristocracy had been fierce and martial in its day, a race of great hunters and unsurpassable conquerors. The traditions told of the mighty capital called the Great City Shang, built by the Shang king Pan Kêng about 1300 B.C., and of the human sacrifices practiced by the Shang nobles in their terrible rites. But, so the stories went, the Shang had grown fat and lazy and drunken, easy prey for the puritanical Chou rulers who finally overthrew them.

The Shang themselves, according to these late accounts, had made an end to an earlier dynasty, the Hsia, which had grown decadent after a long rule. The traditional dates for the reign of the Hsia were 1989-1558 B.C. according to one system, 1994-1523 B.C. after another, 2205-1765 B.C. following a third. The founder of the dynasty had been a great and wise ruler named Yü, who had received the throne as a reward for his services to mankind. Before him had ruled the Five Sovereigns, whose most celebrated representative was Huang Ti, the Yellow Emperor. Huang Ti, who reigned about a hundred years, starting in 2800 B.C., had "established everywhere the order for the sun, the moon, and the stars." Still earlier were the Three August Ones, Fu Hsi, Chu-jung, and Shên-nung, the monarchs of the dawn of time, who had given mankind its basic institutions and skills: agriculture, medicine, the cultivation of silk, the laws of society.

So it was taught, complete with a solemn set of dates that carried Chinese history back beyond even that of Egypt and Sumer. Western historians were tolerantly amused at these pretensions and classed all of Chinese "history" prior to 841 B.C. in the sphere of mythology. Even in China, a group of modern scholars turned on the traditional accounts. They mocked the elaborate genealogies of the ancient monarchs. In a sweeping reaction against the romantic tales of ancient China, these revisionist historians threw all the early dynasties and monarchs under suspicion.

Where was the proof? they demanded. These early kings were no more than myth-shrouded culture heroes, they said; the so-called "authentic" documents of Shang and Hsia times were invented by poets of the Chou Dynasty and were given retroactive existence purely for the sake of enhancing Chinese prestige. The truth was, they said, that nothing reliable was known of Chinese history before the middle of the Chou period, and it was foolishness to waste time making lists of imaginary kings who had lived an impossibly long time ago.

The new historical order was violent and total. Older Chinese scholars clung to their dynasties, feebly defending the existence of the Shang and the Hsia. But the young ones were adamant. Particularly after the Chinese Revolution of 1911–12, when modern ways of thought became fashionable, one invited patronizing smiles to talk about Huang Ti, Yü, and the other alleged sovereigns of early China. The Hsia and Shang Dynasties were discarded as unreal, phantoms of poetic imaginations. So far as the historical record could be trusted, only the Chou was acceptable. Whatever political order had existed before the Chou, these rigorous debunkers said, was an unproven quantity. Evidence! Give us evidence! Not simply forged annals but unquestionable proof! Only then would it be possible to accept the old tales of the ancient monarchs and dynasties.

The absence of an archeological record hampered the task of replacing legend with fact. Archeology had never been favored by the Chinese. They were great antiquarians, yes, collecting and treasuring the relics of the past. But the idea of systematically excavating and studying the ancient sites was an alien one to them.

Traditional feelings ran high against excavations. The Chinese ancestor veneration is legendary, and any sort of digging would involve desecration of the graves of someone's ancestors. Disturbing the honored dead would bring grief to the descendants of the interred and might well cause the wrath of the provoked spirits to descend on the impious excavators. The Chinese belief in *feng shui,* the "science of winds and waters," was another hindrance to archeology. This tradition held that the earth had veins through which cleansing winds and waters passed, affecting the course of human events. No large excavation could be begun without first consulting the authorities on *feng shui* to determine whether the local spirits of winds and waters would be injured. This interfered seriously with the construction of railroads in China—and it also blocked archeology. In a country where no one could thrust a spade into the ground without running the risk of offending an ancestor or severing a vein of the earth, the relics of pre-Chou civilization remained hidden.

There was another and severely practical reason for the absence of scientific archeology. Tomb plundering was an established profession in China. Whole villages had long supported themselves by the illegal uncovering and sale of antiquities. Heedless of *feng shui* or angry ancestors, these rough-hewn countrymen worked the ancient burial places like private mines of treasure. Any scholarly looking type who came prowling about was likely to meet with a swift and unpleasant fate, for he posed a threat to the source of supply. The grave robbers efficiently prevented any real archeological work in China for centuries. Peddling their spoils in Peking, they kept the curio dealers well supplied and insured a steady flow of ancient bronzes and porcelains into the hands of the private collectors.

Not only the curio dealers provided an active market for these busy excavators; the apothecaries were interested, too. One of the most useful drugs in the Chinese pharmacopoeia was powdered dragons' bones. A Chinese druggists' guide of the eighteenth century tells us:

Dragons' bones are effective in the diseases of the heart, kidneys, intestines, and liver. They improve vitality. In the case of nervous affections this medicine is particularly recommended to persons suffering from timidity and shyness. Dragons' bones are also helpful to those who are troubled by high blood pressure, and in cases of nightmare, epilepsy, fever, consumption, ulcers, and difficulty in breathing.

A handy medicine, certainly! But what were dragons' bones?

They were the fossilized remains of animals which are now extinct, dug from the yellow earth of northern China: teeth, ribs, leg bones of such creatures as the tapir, the saber-tooth "tiger," and various others, including elephants. Peasants diligently dug up these yellowed bones and sold them to city apothecaries, who ground them to powder for use in expensive medicines.

About 1898 a new source of dragons' bones came to light near the small village of Hsiao T'un, in northern Honan Province, not far from the city of Anyang. Anyang lies about eighty miles north of the Yellow River and about three hundred miles west of the sea, in a district known to be one of the most ancient in China.

Farmers plowing their fields along the banks of the Huan River, which flows directly north of Hsiao T'un, discovered a rich supply of dragons' bones. They were odd, as such bones went, for they were highly polished and covered with unusual notches and T-shaped cracks. A few even bore markings: neat rows of geometrical designs and what looked like pictures. The farmers of Hsiao T'un, without pausing to puzzle over the unlikely presence of inscriptions on dragons' bones, gathered them up and happily carted them off to Peking for sale.

It was not the first time that valuable relics had been found near Anyang. A great storm in A.D. 1079 had split open the earth, uncovering splendid bronze vessels of great antiquity. For centuries thereafter, the people around Anyang had quarried the underground tombs for these bronzes, which were in high demand by collectors. Chinese antiquaries assumed that the Anyang bronzes were of Chou Dynasty date. But these inscribed dragons' bones forced them to take a closer look at the underground treasures of Anyang.

The apothecaries who bought the Anyang bones were troubled by the presence of markings on some of them. Perhaps such bones were not the authentic medicinal item. So they hastily ground them to powder before the customers could see the inexplicable inscriptions. Where the bones were sold in wholesale unpowdered lots to customers, the druggists went to the trouble of scraping the inscriptions off before delivery.

But it happened that the Grand Secretary Wang I-jung, a court official with antiquarian interests, caught sight of some inscribed bones before their markings could be obliterated. He recognized their importance at once. The inscriptions were texts in Chinese—but an incredibly archaic kind of script. Chinese characters had not changed in any fundamental way for at least 2,500 years. These must be older. Their kinship to modern Chinese writing was obvious, and it was even possible to decipher a few words. Clearly this represented an ancestral form of Chinese writing, perhaps even older than Chou Dynasty times.

The news spread. Chinese curio collectors began to seek out the new treasures. Word got around that the inscribed bones were much more valuable than the ordinary dragons' bones. The people of the towns around Anyang hastened to meet the demand. They obligingly added inscriptions to blank bones, imitating the ancient styles so well that many collectors were fooled. By 1914, thousands of inscribed bones were in the hands of collectors and museums, a good many of them fraudulent but a vast number authentic.

Chinese scholars examined the inscriptions in fascination and awe. They quickly determined that they were dealing with the oldest known forms of Chinese script. The characters were basically pictographic: a horse was indicated by a drawing of a horse, a stuck pig by that of a pig skewered by a spear, and so on. Some of the characters were more subtle: the verb "to do" was represented by a drawing of a hand guiding an elephant, and the word for "year" showed a farmer hauling his harvested sheaves from the field. There was no doubt that these texts could be read and understood—and that they had been written in the time of the Shang Dynasty.

The Shang, though, had been relegated to limbo by serious Chinese historians; they had come to regard the dynasty as no more historical than the legendary Yellow Emperor of 2800 B.C., whose reign had supposedly lasted more than a century. Suddenly, awkwardly, a whole archive of Shang inscriptions was at hand. The inscribed bones bore brief texts, never more than sixty words in length, which appeared to be the records of oracular prophecies. Shang Dynasty kings were named—including nearly all those listed in the much-condemned traditional accounts of the period!

The oracle bones of Anyang had rescued the Shang Dynasty

from oblivion. No longer could Shang be scorned as a myth. Chinese traditionalists who had seen cold-hearted moderns junk thousands of years of accepted history now rejoiced as a substantial segment of the discarded tradition returned to respectability. And Western historians, long skeptical of the claimed antiquity of Chinese civilization, were dismayed to learn that there had been a Shang Dynasty after all.

Though the famous bones were discovered in 1898 and translated within a few years, decades went by before the sites of Anyang received their first scientific examination. Political difficulties caused much of the delay: the establishment of the Chinese Republic in 1912 was followed by years of anarchy, with local warlords ruling in virtual independence of the central government, and hardly had the Nationalist Kuomintang party established some sort of control over the country than the newly organized Communists began a civil war against it. Even in more tranquil times, though, it had been difficult to organize any archeological expeditions in China because of the prevailing popular antipathy toward large-scale excavations, and this, too, helped keep scientists away from Anyang.

Some foreign archeologists and paleontologists had managed to carry on work in China, however. Fossil teeth of ancient man had turned up in the apothecary shops, and European paleontologists excited by these finds had received permission to excavate at a site called Dragon Bone Hill, near Peking. There, in 1927, they unearthed the first known relic of what was called Peking Man, or *Sinanthropus,* an apelike human form some 500,000 years old. This discovery aroused considerable interest overseas in the archeology of China. At the Freer Gallery of Art of the Smithsonian Institution, Associate Curator Carl Whiting Bishop attempted to launch an expedition to work at Anyang. Bishop alone could make no headway; but a young Chinese archeologist named Li Chi, who had been studying anthropology at Harvard and then had joined Bishop's staff at the Freer, helped to get the project under way.

Li was one of the many scientists exported by Republican China for education abroad, in the wholesale attempt to carry China into the modern world after its long slumber under the

Manchu emperors. After taking his doctorate at Harvard in 1923 and working briefly at the Freer Gallery, Li returned to China and in 1928 became Head of the Archeology Section of the Institute of History and Philology of the Academia Sinica, the Chinese national research body. That permitted him at last to begin work at Anyang. Late in 1928, a seventeen-day preliminary excavation was made there, and in 1929 the work began in full scale, under the joint auspices of the Academia Sinica and the Freer Gallery.

The archeologists were faced with extraordinary problems. The winters were too cold and the summers too hot for any kind of archeological work, so the excavation had to be carried out in two-month bursts in spring and autumn. But those were the windy seasons, when knife-sharp gusts ripped across the yellow earth, raising blinding clouds that made it impossible to see more than twenty feet. The wind erosion not only made life difficult for the goggle-wearing archeologists but had badly affected the stratification of the sites, so that it was a challenging task to arrive at some meaningful interpretation of what was found. At sites like Jericho or Ras Shamra, where one culture's deposits lay relatively neatly above those of its predecessor, determining relative ages was not nearly the task it was at Anyang, where heavy cultural objects tended to sink through the shifting sand to strata of earlier periods.

Nature's obstacles were not the only ones. Poverty-stricken peasants, furious at this invasion of their time-hallowed plundering grounds, menaced the archeologists constantly. Li Chi received threats of assassination from a "defense association" dedicated to the preservation of Anyang's relics for the profit of the local peasantry. Government soldiers were assigned to protect the archeologists, and there were no casualties. The villagers resorted to a redoubled campaign of grave robbing in the hopes of snatching what they could before the archeologists removed it. Dr. H. G. Creel of the University of Chicago, who was present during the Academia Sinica's excavations at Anyang, provides this description of the mood of the time:

As a result of the official ban on digging, the grave robbers have now developed a method of nocturnal operation. . . . To prevent them from prospecting in the daytime is almost impossible. They use an instrument something like a post-hole digger, and when this brings up a peculiar type of "pounded earth," they know that they have located an ancient grave. In preparation for digging they assemble fifty or sixty men, all with the greatest secrecy. After nightfall this band, all armed with guns, proceeds to the chosen spot. A few of them dig; the rest, taking advantage of any natural cover, or devising some slight protection, form an armed ring about the scene of operations. Work proceeds feverishly and the entire tomb is gutted before morning. As compared with their abject poverty there is a fortune for each of these peasants at stake in their enterprise. If any attempt is made to interfere with them they will shoot to kill.

Such private excavations caused an irreparable scientific loss. Bronze vessels and inscribed bones came to the Peking curio markets without having been recorded in their original strata. Though many of these ended in the possession of museums, others disappeared into the hands of rich private collectors, who permitted no further examination. The pillaging peasants naturally ignored anything that did not seem to be of immediate resale value; they ripped bronze fittings from ancient chariots, kicking the useless wooden frameworks to bits, and scattered the bones of Shang skeletons in a deliberate attempt to keep the dead from taking vengeance.

Plagued by the weather, the local banditry, the protests of Chinese traditionalists, and the activities of these looters, the archeologists still managed to continue their labors at Anyang almost without a break. The 1930 season had to be canceled when the area became a battleground of the civil war, but Li Chi and his collaborators returned in 1931, 1932, and 1933.

The 1934 season saw such a sinister rise in the rate of private digging that it began to appear as if the looters would enter every Shang Dynasty tomb before the archeologists could carry out the necessary studies. In the 1929–33 seasons, the excavators had concentrated on the dwellings of the Shang people, not the tombs. Meanwhile one tomb after another had been vandalized by the nocturnal looters. So far not one Shang tomb had been properly excavated, nor had any Shang bronzes been unearthed under controlled conditions. "Most important of all," wrote Dr. Creel, we had virtually no reliable data on the racial characteristics of the Shang people. Hundreds of accurately datable skeletons had been destroyed ruthlessly; not one had been preserved. Were the bronze-using Shang aristocrats Mongoloid, descendants of the Neolithic inhabitants of northeast China? Or were they, as some maintained, alien invaders from the West? We could not say. And the pillars of the grave-robbing industry sent word to the excavators saying that while their activities in the dwelling-sites (which yield little that is saleable) had been tolerated, one attempt to go beyond this and excavate tombs would be the signal for a quiet shot in the back for each of the scholars directing the work.

The archeologists appealed to the national government. From Chiang Kai-shek came a vehement telegram to the local authorities at Anyang, banning all private digging and ordering complete protection for the scientists. This had some effect, apparently. Dr. Li hired three hundred workmen and set about the excavation of a large field of Shang graves. By the end of the spring season of 1935, more than eleven hundred unquestionable Shang skeletons were recovered, and more than three hundred Shang tombs had been scientifically studied, four of them huge royal sepulchers. The evidence of the oracle bones had been at last corroborated in detail by the spade.

The Japanese invasion of North China put an end to all archeology at Anyang in the summer of 1937. The Institute of History and Philology packed its collections and began a retreat that eventually brought it to southwestern China. As the Anyang treasures were hauled hither and thither to keep them from falling into Japanese hands, much of the archeological material was lost: stratified soil samples, potsherds, charcoal remains, unpublished field notes. Despite these catastrophes, the Chinese archeological journals managed to get into print reproductions of the oracle-bone inscriptions excavated between 1928 and 1937, though it was impossible to offer an adequate scientific publication of the full Anyang findings.

The end of the Japanese occupation in 1945 brought new difficulties for the Academia Sinica archeologists, for now Anyang and its environs fell to the Chinese Communists. The long civil war reached its climax in 1949 with the expulsion of the remaining Nationalists, and as Chiang Kai-shek's supporters departed for Taiwan they took with them as much of the national archeological holdings as possible. Li Chi was among those who fled; he became the head of the Department of Anthropology and Archaeology at National Taiwan University in 1950. Since then, he has presided over the gradual publication of the surviving material excavated under his supervision at Anyang before the Japanese invasion.

The situation was a tragedy for Chinese archeology. Much of the Shang material and most of the trained archeologists were on Taiwan, while Anyang and the other Shang sites remained still not fully excavated, a world away on the mainland. The Communist government of China, though, saw fit to encourage a resurgence of national feeling that included a great interest in the monuments of the past. The Archaeological Institute of the Peking Academy of Sciences was organized in 1950, and soon new excavations were under way at Anyang. The work has continued since that time, though it is not always easy for Westerners to find out what is being discovered. Apparently the problem of private enterprise in tomb robbing no longer exists, now that Communist discipline has been exerted even in outlying provinces, and some of the discoveries of recent years have been of exceptional interest.

Today no one suggests that the Shang Dynasty is mythological. It has been restored to its place in Chinese history, and for once the seemingly credulous poetic legends turned out to have a surprisingly accurate basis in fact. Solid evidence, in the form of excavated towns and tombs and most spectacularly in the form of written records, shows that the Shang really did exist, a sophisticated and highly advanced culture with many puzzling aspects.

Who were the Shang? Where did they come from? How did they become so skillful at the casting of bronze vessels? To whom, if anybody, did they owe their use of writing? These are some of the Shang mysteries. Even though the Chinese archeological record is no longer a blank, it has raised as many problems as it has settled, and Shang civilization is one of the outstanding challenges to the archeologists who are attempting to fit together an image of the world of the past.

The awkward thing about the Shang Dynasty as we know it

today is the absence of its preliminary stages. The oldest Shang inscriptions show a system of writing already complex and highly evolved. The earliest known Shang bronzes display breathtaking mastery of technique. We see no groping, no hesitant fumbling toward perfection.

This has led archeologists from the West to make the unkind suggestion that Shang culture was not indigenous to China. Against a global backgound, it can be seen that the Shang were latecomers to civilization; Egypt's Pyramids were twelve centuries old before the first Shang town was built, and the Sumerians had perfected their cuneiform writing a millennium and a half before the oldest known Shang oracle bones were carved. Therefore, the argument goes, everything the Shang knew was borrowed from the Near East. An extreme version of this position holds that the Shang themselves were conquerors of non-Chinese stock who made their way eastward about 1500 B.C. and superimposed their culture on the primitive Chinese peasantry they found in the Yellow River area.

China's archeologists have been quick to oppose this school of thought, insisting on the fundamentally East Asian origin of the Shang. Until the 1920's, their viewpoint had the hollow ring of patriotic fervor, which is never a good substitute for scientific evidence. There had been so little real archeology done in China that the country's whole prehistoric past was a blank. The discovery of *Sinanthropus* in 1927 proved that man had inhabited China hundreds of thousands of years ago; and then the Anyang excavations provided the proof that Chinese Neolithic culture was a native product. By 1935, when skeletons of undoubted Shang period were scientifically unearthed, it became clear that the Shang themselves were of the Chinese racial stock, not intruders from the Near East.

There had certainly been contact between China and the Near East in prehistoric times, the Chinese archeologists admitted. Chinese pottery of pre-Shang date showed definite kinship to pottery of Iran and Syria. More significantly, a common decorative motif on Shang bronzes and wood carvings recovered at Anyang was a human figure wrestling with two animals. This was the standard Mesopotamia portrayal of the Hercules-like hero Gil-

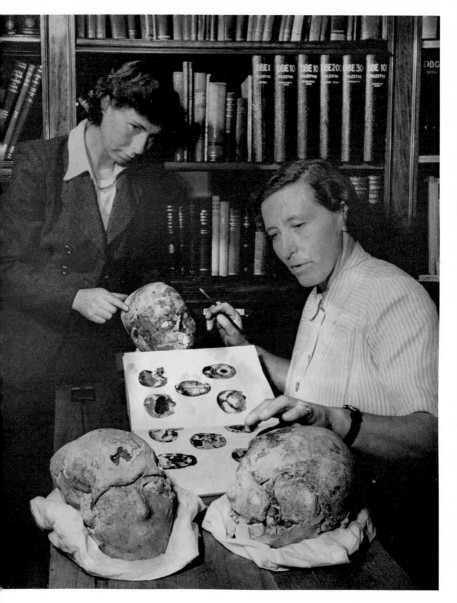

Dr. Kathleen Kenyon examines sculptured Neolithic heads from Jericho, assisted by Cecil Western. *Courtesy* National Geographic Magazine © *National Geographic Society*

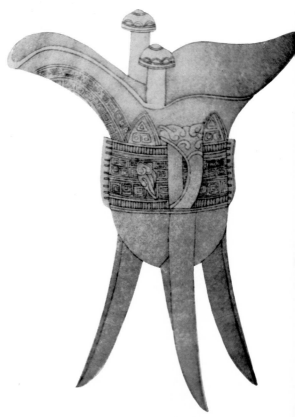

(Above, left) Shang jade knife with bronze hilt. *Collection of Dr. Arthur M. Sackler* (Below) Shang bronze tripod vessel. *Photo from collection of the author*

The main, base wall of Zimbabwe. *Courtesy of the American Museum of Natural History*

Temple of Quetzalcoatl, Teotihuacan. *Courtesy of the University Museum, Univ. of Pa.*

gamesh, which persisted in the art of Iran, Greece, and Egypt in a variety of forms. Dr. Li Chi concedes that the Anyang pattern "is evidently a degenerated version of the famous Hero and Beast motif, which . . . originated in Mesopotamia." He goes on to cite other instances of contact between Near East and Far East in the second millennium B.C. But his conclusion is that which most Chinese authorities and many Western ones accept today:

The nature of such contact could scarcely be inferred from the above evidences; it may have been a very remote one resulting in partial imitations, such as most of the instances cited actually were. The real foundation of the Shang culture was still in the Asiatic East, which also gave rise to and inspired the major art tradition of the whole Pacific basin.

If Shang culture is native to China, then, where are its developmental stages to be found? "Like every other craft and institution," Dr. Li writes, "the bronze industry of China never was a gift from heaven; it emerged gradually and developed step by step." But the signs of this gradual emergence have eluded the archeologists so far. Shang culture appears virtually full-grown on the archeological horizon, and the hope that developmental stages will be unearthed has remained so far unfulfilled.

A fair amount is known about the cultures that immediately preceded the Shang in China. The traditional records, written in Chou Dynasty times, tell of a dynasty called the Hsia that ruled until the Shang conquest. Many shadowy references to the Hsia are found in Chou texts, but they are totally absent from any of the Shang oracle-bone inscriptions and from the inscriptions on the Shang bronze vessels. Whoever the Hsia may be, it is safe to say that the Shang did not know them by that name. The 1925 opinion of the Swedish archeologist J. G. Andersson was that "the Hsia remains entirely legendary as, so far, no archeological material has been found to support the scanty historical data." Nothing in more than forty years of further work has come to light to upset that verdict.

But there were at least two distinct Chinese cultural groups in the pre-Shang period: the Yang-shao or Painted Pottery culture, and the Lung-shan or Black Pottery culture. Attempts have been made to identify the Yang-shao people as the Hsia, but without much conviction. Since they lacked a knowledge of writing, it will probably never be possible to determine what they called themselves and whether they are the Hsia of the traditional annals.

J. G. Andersson, a Swedish mining engineer who went to China in 1914 as a technical adviser to the Chinese government and remained to do archeological work, discovered the Yang-shao culture in 1922. It was the first evidence of a Neolithic Chinese culture. Within a year's time, Andersson had found deposits of the Yang-shao type in dozens of sites stretching for hundreds of miles along the Yellow River Valley of North China, from Sinkiang in the west to Manchuria in the east.

The Yang-shao people were farmers who planted their crops in the rich, fertile yellow soil known as loess, whose color gives its name to the silt-choked Yellow River. Avoiding the highlands, they clustered near the Yellow River and its tributaries along a broad east-west band. They raised millet, and perhaps rice, and lived in villages of round and oblong huts with sunken floors. The chief identifying characteristic of the Yang-shao culture (named for the town where it was first identified) it its exquisite pottery: a fine red ware ornamented with painted motifs of spirals or circles. This pottery, made not on a potter's wheel but by the painstaking building up and smoothing of coil after coil of clay, amazed Andersson with its beauty and elegance.

When information on the Yang-shao ware reached Europe, specialists pointed out its resemblance to certain pottery forms of Afghanistan, Iran, and western Turkestan, dating from about 3000 B.C. They used this as evidence of the Western origin of Chinese civilization, and some authorities went so far as to suggest that the Chinese themselves were Western in origin, migrating eastward en masse some time in the third millennium B.C. Today such views are rarely put forth, and the undeniable link between Yang-shao pottery and the wares of western Asia is explained simply as a case of some kind of diffusion of influences, without any great significance.

The one place in North China where no Yang-shao sites were found was the province of Shantung, in the east. This seemed baffling; as Li Chi pointed out, "Shantung is China's Holy Land, not merely for the reason that Confucius was born there; it was also, as many historians would testify, the cultural center of China in the first millennium B.C. And, what is even more important, it was most probably the homeland where the culture of the Shang Dynasty had its early growth."

The problem of prehistoric culture in Shantung was answered in 1930 when the young archeologist Wu Gin Ding, a pupil of Li Chi, unearthed the first examples of the prevailing culture of northeastern Neolithic China at the town of Lung-shan. This, too, was a farming culture of small villages on low knolls or river terraces. Like the Yang-shao people, the Lung-shan farmers lived in round or rectangular houses whose foundations were sunk in the earth. They domesticated the pig, cow, and goat, raised millet, and, near the coast, depended heavily on shellfish to supplement their diet.

Lung-shan pottery is wholly unlike that of the Yang-shao culture. The wheel-turned pots are extraordinarily thin-walled, sometimes reaching thicknesses of less than an eighth of an inch. The best Lung-shan pottery bears no decorations and is a lustrous black in color, burnished to a high gloss.

Determining the relationship in time between Yang-shao and Lung-shan and between both cultures and the Shang has been difficult and controversial, but certain general patterns have emerged. Whenever the three types of cultures are found at the same site, the Lung-shan is always above the Yang-shao, and the Shang above the Lung-shan. Nowhere are Lung-shan deposits found above Shang or Yang-shao above Lung-shan. So it appears that a Painted-Pottery–Black-Pottery–Shang sequence of development can be accepted.

Not all the strata are so neat, of course, nor do the three cultures overlap in many places. An additional complication is the existence of several stages of the Painted Pottery culture, with substantial variations between the eastern and western sites. Andersson eventually divided the Painted Pottery culture into six main periods, dating from 2500 to 500 B.C., indicating that in some parts of China the Yang-shao people continued to live as a separate cultural group long after the Shang Dynasty was succeeded by the Chou. In north-central China, though, the Painted Pottery culture gave way to Shang about 1500 B.C., according to Andersson's system. (No carbon-14 dates have yet been calculated for China, so all chronology is necessarily approximate.)

The sites where Shang deposits are found above those of Yang-shao or Lung-shan types are, naturally, those where archeologists have hoped to find some information on the early development of the Shang. So far they have learned nothing illuminating; at each site is a sudden overlay of fully evolved Shang. The transitional phases remain missing. Abruptly the Shang are there: casters of bronze, inscribers of oracle bones, differing from the earlier cultures in every meaningful way.

Some attempts have been made to show that the Shang evolved from the Lung-shan. The Lung-shan or Black Pottery sites are found in the northeast, the traditional place of Shang origin. Some of the Shang bronze vessels seem to be modeled after types of Lung-shan pottery, notably a three-lobed goblet. Stone axes of Lung-shan style were also used by the Shang. Oracle bones of the Shang sort were found in older Lung-shan sites.

But the Lung-shan were fundamentally different from the Shang in too many ways. The Shang characteristics are the use of metals, the possession of a highly developed writing system, the employment of war chariots, the custom of tomb burial, and the technique of stone carving. None of these are found among the Lung-shan. And Shang pottery, a rough, coarse ware, is poor stuff beside the gleaming Lung-shan work.

Until the evidence appears, the origins of Shang must remain a mystery to us. As it now appears, the charioteers of Shang erupted onto the peaceful central Chinese plains about 1500 B.C. from some unknown homeland, bringing with them a fully developed Bronze Age culture. Imposing themselves on the Black Pottery people of the northeast and the Painted Pottery people of the west, they established a military dictatorship that lasted five hundred years and left a permanent imprint on the Chinese way of life. The skeletal evidence tells us that they were of Chinese racial stock, so we can no longer accept the idea that they were roaming Aryan adventurers from the West, as was so often suggested before the Anyang excavations. The developmental sites of the Shang, when they are finally discovered, will almost certainly lie somewhere in eastern China.

The Western origin of Shang culture, however, is harder to disprove. The Orientalist Max Loehr, discussing the Anyang bronzes in 1949, wrote, "Metallurgy seems to have been brought to China from outside. Whence, is an open question; but whatever the sources were, the way led via Siberia and possibly Eastern Turkestan." J. G. Andersson, who sought in vain to find bronze in the most ancient Yang-shao deposits, found none earlier than 1300 B.C., well after the arrival of the Shang. Carl W. Bishop of the Freer Gallery expressed the opinion in 1934 that "the Bronze Age civilization, as an integrated complex, reached China by way of the Central Asiatic steppe belt." At present, though, there has been little excavation done in Siberia. Bronze-working cultures existed there in prehistoric times, but it is not yet possible to show whether they are ancestral to Shang China or descended from it. Dr. Li Chi and his colleagues on Taiwan feel strongly that the Shang culture evolved within China, totally separate from the Yang-shao and perhaps kin to the Lung-shan, receiving influences from outside but not borrowing fundamentally from foreign civilizations. The Chinese Communist archeologists, with their extreme nationalism, naturally refuse to accept the possibility that the wondrous flowering of Shang was the work of outsiders. The feeling of many younger authorities in the West is well expressed by the British Orientalist, William Willetts, who wrote:

The only reason we have for supposing that earlier phases of the history of writing and of bronze art did not occur in China, as far as I can see, is that they are as yet undiscovered. Field archaeology in that country is still much too backward for us to be able to make reasonable inferences based on what it has *not* brought to light, and the origins of the Chinese Bronze Age, I conclude, are as likely to be found there as anywhere else.

The debate over the origins of Shang bronze working should not be allowed to obscure one vital point. What is surprising about the Shang bronzes is not so much their mere presence in China at that time—bronze had been worked in the Near East many centuries earlier—but that they are unsurpassed works of art. The Shang bronze vessels are without equal. No artists before or since, within China or without, have ever matched the technique that is displayed so stunningly by the Shang pieces.

They were ritual vessels of prescribed shapes, cast to celebrate specific occasions: a great victory, a heroic exploit, the awarding of a feudal fief, or the like. They were cast usually in honor of a specific ancestor, whose name would be inscribed on the vessel. At the regular sacrificial feasts in honor of these ancestors, each Shang family would bring forth its bronzes for the pouring of libations and the bearing of meat offerings; probably the vessels were carefully stored under close guard the rest of the year. When a Shang noble died, bronzes accompanied him to his tomb, and so many of these remarkable vessels were buried that the black-market excavation and peddling of them was a profitable Chinese industry for nearly a thousand years. As a result of this lamentable pilferage, virtually every major museum of the world has a fine collection of Shang bronzes, and many are in private collections. About 15,000 authentic pieces are known, and untold thousands of imitations.

There are about fifty general types of vessels. Some two dozen of these are known to collectors by their names, as found in inscriptions on them. The type called *ting,* for example, was a squat cooking pot on legs; the *ku* was a tapering goblet for wine; the *chüeh,* one of the strangest, a three-legged drinking vessel with weird hornlike excrescences. The fanciful shapes of the Shang pieces were enhanced by the unsettling baroque ornamentation that on some examples covers every square inch without a feeling of clutter. These are nightmare designs, ogres' faces arranged in geometrical rhythms, eerie coiling and shifting patterns that strike frightening notes of mingled terror and beauty. The most common motif is known as the *t'ao-t'ieh,* which can just barely be recognized as the stylized representation of some ghastly mask, whose snout and horns and staring eyes refuse to obey the ordinary laws of perspective. Beaks, tusks, fangs lurk in unexpected corners of these Shang designs. One sees the savagery that lay not far beneath the surface in this civilization.

The craftsmanship of the Shang bronzesmiths is the despair of imitators. H. G. Creel chose at random a vessel of the *ku* type, "not of the finest quality," for examination. It was probable, he noted, that every Shang family of any means had one or more of this type, and they must have been produced "in considerable numbers, almost as a factory industry." Yet the delicate traceries of the goblet remained sharp and clear even under a magnifying glass:

Its corners are corners; if a projection was intended, even for the tiniest fraction of an inch, it projects. Most of the channels cast in its surface, making up the tracery, are one thirty-second of an inch or less in width. But these channels are not merely troughs, grooves of any sort. The walls of the grooves go back straight, for about three sixty-fourths of an inch, until they reach the bottom. Then there is a square corner, and the bottom of the groove runs quite flat to the point where it meets the other wall, again in a square corner. In other words, a profile of these grooves would show, not a curve, but three sides of a rectangle. If one compares these vessels with some of the modern bronzes cast in China in the attempt to duplicate them the contrast is no less than pitiable.

The Shang smiths had several methods for producing these wonders. The earliest known technique involved making piece molds of clay, fitted together at the edges by dowels. Six to twelve of these sectional molds were needed for a single goblet or bowl, apparently. Many piece molds have been recovered at Anyang, but the most important discovery was made under Communist auspices in an early Shang site at the modern city of Chengchow. There, in 1950, deposits of the Anyang type were uncovered, with less elegant artifacts in developing Shang style below them—one of the first valuable finds offering information on the evolutionary stages of Shang culture. In 1955, more extensive excavations revealed that a Shang city more than a mile square had existed there; unfortunately most of the site lay under the modern city and was inaccessible, but some digging was carried out in the western suburbs.

During this 1955 dig, two bronze-casting workshops were cleared. Small conical pits, their sides smoothed and hardened, were sunk in the floor, their rims blackened and surrounded by bits of slag. Bucket-shaped clay crucibles had been used for re-

[73]

fining the ore. Earthenware section molds were scattered about, bearing the negative patterns of typical bronze designs. Molten metal was poured into these molds after they had been assembled, and the patterns were impressed by direct contact. But this direct-casting method was not suitable for the finest and most delicate designs, and most of the great Shang bronzes of later days were made by the much more tractable *cire perdue* or "lost-wax" technique.

In this process, used by metalworking cultures in many parts of the world, a wax model of the intended piece is prepared around a clay core. Designs to appear on the finished piece are carved or stamped on the wax. Then, once the soft wax has received the decorative pattern, an outer coating of clay is applied, brushed on with great care so that it will mate exactly to the outlines in the wax. Some holes are left through which the wax can later escape.

The finished mold is a sandwich of wax, bearing the design, between inner and outer layers of clay. Now the mold is placed in an oven. The heat melts the wax, which runs off, and molten bronze is poured into the empty space left between the clay walls. This must be done artfully, so that the metal runs into every fine line of the mold. When the casting is complete the outer mold and the core are broken away from the cool bronze, and all that remains is to trim away extraneous projections of metal and finish the vessel with tools. As H. G. Creel comments:

It is in connection with this finishing that the superiority of the ancient Chinese craftsmen over many of their best rivals elsewhere appears. There must certainly have been little "necks" of bronze, representing the holes through which the molten metal was poured, which had to be cut and smoothed off. But it is the opinion of connoisseurs that except for this the casting was so perfect, in the case of the finer pieces, at least, that no retouching was necessary. We think of the work of Benvenuto Cellini as superlatively fine, but those who have examined his castings say that they are full of spots where, the metal having failed to fill out the mould, metal "plugs" have subsequently been inserted and finished off with tools. It is agreed that while a very few of the best living craftsmen in Europe or America, aided by all the resources of modern science and technology, may be able to equal the casting of the Shang bronze workers, they can do no better.

Pyramid of the Sun, Teotihuacan. *Courtesy of the Mexican National Tourist Council*

The great calendar stone of the Aztecs.   *Courtesy of the Mexican National Tourist Council*

Carved wood figure of a "bird man," Easter Island.   *Courtesy of the American Museum of Natural History*

Wood "Rongo-rongo board," with pictograph writing, Easter Island. *Courtesy of the American Museum of Natural History*

Stone heads outside Rano Raraku crater, Easter Island. *Courtesy of the American Museum of Natural History*

By any standards the Shang bronzes are extraordinary achievements. So, too, is the Shang system of writing, as it has come down to us in the oracle-bone inscriptions. Though scarcely the oldest writing system of mankind, it is certainly the most durable. Every basic principle of modern Chinese writing grows from roots in the Shang. Though many new characters have been added, and the old ones greatly modified, Shang writing is close enough to modern Chinese to permit ready decipherment of more than a third of the 5,000 known Shang characters.

A Chinese legend dating back to Chou times credits the invention of writing to one Ts'ang Chieh, said to have had four eyes and to have taken the idea of a written language from the scratchings of birds' claws upon sand. Before this, a crude system of knotted cords was mankind's only method of recording events. "Upon the achievement of his task," a biographical account informs us, "the sky rained grain and evil spirits mourned by night."

Ts'ang Chieh was a contemporary of the Yellow Emperor and gave China her writing system about 2600 B.C., according to the traditional tales. Whatever the truth of those stories, the cold archeological fact is that nothing is known of the early stages of Chinese writing. When the earliest Shang oracle bones are examined, dating from 1300 B.C., they reveal a system of writing already mature.

The earliest Chinese writing must have been pictographic: the word for "bird" was a picture of a bird, the word for "house" a schematic house, and so on. But pictography falls short of the ideal script, particularly in its handling of verbs. "To dig" may be represented by a picture of a spade, and "to quarrel" by a sketch of three women in one house, but the script is beginning to get several removes away from pure picture writing and is developing a symbolic shorthand for ideas. Unpictorial concepts like "historian" and "father-in-law" require more complex characters. And the nature of the Chinese language itself forced modifications in the system. Chinese is a language of one-syllable words built on a few basic sound patterns, and there are not enough syllables to go around. A single sound, then, may have to bear a host of meanings, and in the written language each of these meanings would require a different character. The Shang word *shih,* for example, could refer to a type of house or to the scorekeeper in an archery contest, among other things. The character for *shih*-as-house consisted of a dome-shaped line surrounding the character for another word pronounced *shih,* and meant "a word meaning house and pronounced *shih."* This deviated far from the original pictographic idea by admitting a phonetic element. In modern Chinese, many characters are formed on such a principle, one component offering a clue to the meaning of the word, the other a hint of its sound.

In this fashion the Shang built up an elaborate script. Its principles were basically those that underlay Mesopotamian cuneiform, but its characters were wholly different—a situation that has been used to support both the idea that the Chinese borrowed writing from the Sumerians and that they invented it independently. Probably some intermediate case is true: that the concept of picture writing, like the heroic motif of Gilgamesh, made its way eastward to China, perhaps at second or third hand, and was adopted by the Shang for their own purposes.

The only Shang writing that has come down to us is found on the oracle bones, except for some extremely brief inscriptions on the bronzes. No Shang works of literature or history have survived, because they were written on such perishable materials as silk and bamboo, and also quite likely because they were destroyed by the Chou conquerors after 1000 B.C. The Shang character for "book," still in use, shows strips of wood or bamboo tied by a loop of string, but no such Shang books are known to exist today.

The oracle bones, though, are plentiful. For a long time archeologists were not sure of the chronological relationship between these inscribed bones and the tomb bronzes; and Anyang excavators opened more than a thousand tombs without finding a reliable link. But in 1931 a storage pit at the village of Hsiao T'un yielded many inscribed bones in close association with bronze tools and weapons of Shang type, showing that the two cultural developments were contemporary. Since that time storage pits have been the chief source of the bones; one pit at Hsiao T'un produced seven tortoise carapaces whose inscriptions bore the name of the twenty-sixth Shang king and afforded much information on the methods of the Shang oracles. This group of shells seemed to have been an archive deliberately filed below ground for storage. Another pit eighteen feet deep contained 17,906 pieces of bone and shell, most of them inscribed; this was evidently a refuse dump rather than a library.

The Shang diviners used the polished bones of goat, ox, and deer shoulder-blades in the early years of the dynasty but later came to prefer the shells of large tortoises. The species used was unknown to science before the Anyang excavations and was given the name of *Testudo anyangensis*. It is thought to be extinct today and to have flourished in Shang times only in southern China, beyond the Yangtze River. The Shang domain itself extended only through the Yellow River basin, and the Yangtze appears to have been its southern border. The presence of these southern tortoises in huge numbers at Anyang, then, indicates the likelihood that the Chinese states of the south were Shang vassals that sent tribute of shells, or at the least that there was heavy trade between Shang and the south.

The bones or shells were carefully prepared for oracular use. They were filed and polished until smooth and rounded, and all projections were sawed off. Shallow pits were bored in various places along the backs of the bones. The ceremonies of divination were conducted by members of a small caste of official diviners, whose power in the Shang realm must have been great. To obtain information from the gods about the pattern of future events, the diviners applied hot bronze points to the prepared shells until they cracked. By examining the networks of cracks they read the future just as palmists decipher the message in a furrowed hand.

Basically there were two answers: yes or no, favorable or unfavorable, fortunate or unfortunate. The diviner could control the answer to some degree by preparing the bone in such a way as to produce a certainly positive or certainly negative oracle. It has always been useful for diviners to be able to produce the answers the prince wishes to hear, or to shape the divine responses to fit the most probable course of future events. Many of the Shang bones bear only the pattern of cracks, but at some point it became customary to inscribe the question on the bone and sometimes the answer, as well, or even a later comment on the success of the prophecy.

The questions deal with matters of warfare, weather, ritual, and agriculture. Will it rain tonight? Will there be a good harvest this year? Is tomorrow an auspicious day to do battle? Do the ancestors require sacrifices tonight? This is a typical inscription:

> Day *keng tzŭ,* oracle taken, *Cheng* [diviner's name] asking, tomorrow, *hsin ch'ou,* will the weather be fine? asking, tomorrow, *hsin ch'ou,* will the weather not be fine?
> The king examined and said, this evening it will rain, tomorrow, *hsin ch'ou,* it will be fine.
> In that night rain was granted, but on *hsin ch'ou* it was fine.

Late in the Shang period, it became customary to consult the oracles on nearly every decision, no matter how minor. This may have kept the corps of diviners needlessly busy, but it also supplied modern archeology with information about the minute details of Shang life—the names of kings, the system of succession to the throne (from brother to brother within the same generation before passing to the next), the crops raised, the size of armies, and much else. The yes-or-no nature of the answers required that the questions be put in detailed form: not "How large an army shall be sent?" but "Shall an army of five thousand men be sent?"

We know that the Shang nobles were great hunters. The excavations at Anyang unearthed the remains of many wild animals, from monkeys to whales. The bones of bears, tigers, tapirs, leopards, rhinoceroses, elephants, and other creatures were found. That these were taken by Shang hunters is proven by the numerous oracular inscriptions having to do with the prospects for the chase:

> Divine on the day *Wu-wu, Ku* [the diviner] made the inquiry, we are going to hunt at *Ch'iu,* any capture?
> Hunting on this day, we actually captured:
> Tigers, one
> Deer, forty
> Foxes, one hundred and sixty-four
> Hornless deer, one hundred and fifty-nine.

This passion for hunting was almost certainly confined to the aristocracy. At the broad base of the Shang pyramid was the peasantry, toiling in the fields, raising millet and wheat and some rice, and living as it had lived since time immemorial and would go on living for thousands of years more. These peasants clustered in villages lying near their fields and were remote both geographically and economically from the high-walled cities where dwelled the roistering tiger-hunting nobility and the skilled artisans who served them.

Weapons of bronze had placed that nobility in its seat of power. Armed with bronze-tipped arrows and wielding long-shafted bronze halberds, Shang charioteers must have had an easy victory over the Hsia, their traditional predecessors as rulers of the Yellow River basin. Terrifying bronze-helmeted warriors roared through the towns, drawn in chariots by fierce, snarling horses and perhaps backed up by a heavy cavalry of elephants. It would have been no contest.

Midway through their time of supremacy, the Shang built a mighty capital at Anyang. Contemporary inscriptions call it the Great City Shang. Construction began in the fifteenth year of the reign of P'an Kêng, according to the traditional chronology, and this is variously dated between 1384 and 1300 B.C.*

The site was well chosen. The city rose on a promontory where the river curved to create a natural moat on the east, the north, and part of the western front. An earthen wall protected the rest of the city, and beyond lay a flat, broad plain on which an advancing army would be clearly visible. A range of nearly impassable mountains encircling the city at a distance of some seventeen miles on the west completed the natural fortifications.

Here rose a vast city that was to be the Shang capital for nearly three centuries. The foundations of its buildings were of *hang-t'u,* rammed earth, pounded down so hard that thousands of years of weathering have not entirely eroded it. Timber pillars supported roofs or large beams. The houses of the nobles were

* The earliest date comes from orthodox Chinese historical works. A middle chronology is derived from a document called the Chu Shu Chi Nien, or Bamboo Books. But in 1927 Wang Kuo-wei, a Chinese historian, showed that the Bamboo Books text was corrupt and reconstructed the original chronology. He gave 1523 to 1027 B.C. as the Shang dates, and these are generally accepted today, with 1300 taken as the time of the founding of the Great City Shang.

awesome; one had a grand hall 26 feet wide by 92 feet long, with a ridgepole 32 feet high bracing the roof. The woodwork of these palaces was in all likelihood decorated with carvings in the same terrifying motifs found on the Shang bronzes. Outer walls were of *hang-t'u,* smooth as glass, solid enough to ring under the blows of the mallets that shaped it.

From this walled metropolis the Shang aristocrats issued on their expeditions of war and the hunt. Within, craftsmen in bronze performed their wonders, and other artisans produced the humble everyday pottery, the arrowheads, the common tools. Little has survived of the Great City Shang but its foundations, however. The most extensive knowledge of Shang artifacts has come from the cemeteries outside the city.

Thousands of tombs are known, some of them awesomely huge and abundant with evidence of Shang savagery. Not only did bronze vessels, figures of stone, carved jades and ivories, and pottery serve as grave-gifts, but human sacrifices accompanied each Shang grandee to the land of unending sleep.

The tombs were completely subterranean, reached by earthen stepped ramps. One particularly fruitful cemetery was discovered at Hsi Pei Kang, three miles northwest of Anyang. Eight tombs of great size were found there, containing treasures of art that had escaped the plunderers. In one tomb was found a trace of the canopy that had covered the royal coffin, made of wood inlaid with mother-of-pearl, ivory, turquoise, and gold foil arranged in the ogre-mask pattern of the bronzes. Another tomb held a more somber array: human skulls, neatly arranged in rows of ten. Human victims had been buried in kneeling positions at the corners of this tomb, their mouths wide open.

Nearby pits contained headless human skeletons. Others held more rows of severed heads. Horses had been buried in pairs, along with the dismantled parts of a chariot. Dogs, monkeys, and deer had been slaughtered at the funeral. In one pit an elephant lay in solitary majesty.

From the village of Wu Kuan came a report of a nearly intact tomb discovered in 1950. It was a rectangular pit 46 feet by 40, with entry ramps on the northern and southern sides. The walls descended straight for 15½ feet; after a step, they descended another 8 feet, and here lay the body of a funeral victim, armed with a bronze halberd so that he might guard the main burial chamber below. Further steps led downward. Grave goods were arranged on each step: jade knives, stone vessels, many bronzes, some pottery. Seventeen men had been buried on the east side, twenty-four women on the west. In pits on the north ramp were the remains of sixteen slaughtered horses. The bodies of dogs, deer, and monkeys lay in the rammed-earth filling of the pit over the burial chamber. In an upper layer were thirty-four human skulls set in rows. Headless human skeletons were found buried in groups of ten in small pits south of the main tomb.

At the village of Ta Ssu K'ung Ts'un, a complete chariot burial was uncovered in 1953. A pit large enough for the chariot and its horses had been dug, with grooves in the earth to take the wheels, the axle, and the shaft. The chariot had been carefully placed in position, its two-horse team slain and placed on either side of the shaft, and the body of the dead warrior himself stretched at full length crosswise in the chariot. The wood of the vehicle had vanished, but its pattern survived even to the thin spokes of the wheels, as impressions against the earth of the pit. Again, there had been human sacrifices.

It is not a pretty picture. Nor were archeologists cheered to find, when they uncovered a Shang factory where awls, arrowheads, and hairpins had been made from bone, that about half the raw material of this workshop consisted of human thigh bones. Life was cheap in Shang China, and ritual terror must have been a part of everyday existence. It is not hard to picture the gruesome pomp of a Shang burial, with hapless servants marching meekly into the open tomb under the supervision of priests whose colorful costumes bore the frightening decorative motifs of nightmare complexity. In one season alone at Anyang, the excavators came upon more than a thousand headless victims of Shang sacrifices. Beauty and ghastly cruelty were not far separated in this strange and alien civilization.

In time retribution came. Sleek and fat, oiled with the blood of myriad sacrifices, the Shang aristocracy lost its grip on China. The oracle-bone inscriptions tell of constant warfare, of rising insurrections in the northwest, the east, the southeast. Armies were dispatched; and still the kings of Shang maintained their gory pomp, their flamboyant hunting expeditions, their splendor and luxury.

The unruly tribes of the southeast appear to have occupied the attention of the Shang troops frequently during the twelfth century B.C. But the real enemy lay elsewhere, in the basin of the Wei River, some three hundred miles west and a hundred miles south of the Great City Shang. There, a confederacy of country-men calling themselves the Chou gathered strength and looked enviously toward the wealthy, comfortable Shang realm in the east.

The Chou people were Chinese, of the same racial stock as the Shang. Chou historians of a later date, rewriting events for the sake of prestige, claimed that the Chou were descended from exiled members of the old Hsia Dynasty, which the Shang had overthrown. This gave a certain air of legitimacy to the Chou overthrow of the Shang. But in fact the Chou were backward countryfolk with no royal ancestors, who may very well have invented both the Hsia Dynasty and their descent from it for purely political reasons.

As their power consolidated, the Chou probably were content to pay tribute to the Shang and humble themselves as vassals. Chou emissaries journeyed to the Shang cities, stared popeyed at their opulence, and returned with tales of wonder—as well as with hard reports on Shang military strength and information on Shang fighting methods. The Chou learned quickly. At first the Shang may have been amused by the pretensions of these country cousins, but soon there was nothing amusing at all about them.

The first Chou ruler whose name is recorded is King Wên, "the Cultured King." In his reign of seven years he laid the ground-work for the conquest of Shang, according to dynastic chronicles that must be reasonably accurate in their general outlines. His son and successor, King Wu, "the Martial King," inherited Wên's blueprint for victory and made it a reality.

In the ninth year of his reign King Wu ventured eastward across the Yellow River, but his attack on Shang was repulsed. Two years later, gathering allies from many tribes who would be glad to see the end of Shang domination, he tried again. His second invasion may have coincided with a time of Shang weakness, or with a Shang expedition to the southeast that left the homeland poorly defended. The official Chou explanation, which we need not credit too seriously, is that the Shang were so sodden with debauchery and drunkenness that they were unable to resist the Chou onslaught.

The end of Shang came in a single battle, now placed in 1027 B.C. Fifty thousand Chou slaughtered 700,000 Shang soldiers, declare the Chou annals without much plausibility. The last of the Shang kings, Chou Hsin, perished in the flames of his extravagant pleasure pavilion, and the warriors of Chou ran freely through the capital of the Shang.

The dynasty was overthrown, but now the conquest had to be secured. The Chou, upstarts out of the west, had a difficult task in establishing their authority over the Shang territories. The only practicable method of administration was a feudal one: Wu, the Chou king, parceled out fiefs to his generals, who would rule semiautonomously, pledging allegiance to the central Chou government. Otherwise it would have been impossible for the central authority to impose its will over the vast conquered area.

The new Chou rulers borrowed from Shang culture in most ways. They adopted Shang writing, Shang art, and Shang laws, regarding themselves as protectors and continuators of the established order. Chou documents show that after the conquest all officials were instructed to follow the ways of the Shang (whom the Chou referred to as the Yin, for reasons unknown to us). We find such statements as these: "Follow the penal laws of Yin, which were right-ordered." "Study the old accomplished men of Yin, that you may establish your heart, and know how to instruct the people." "Employ the ceremonies of Yin and sacrifice in the new city." "Seek out extensively among the traces of the former wise kings of Yin what you may use in protecting and governing the people."

The traces of the former wise kings of Yin included the heir of the dead Shang ruler. King Wu made use of him as a puppet, naming him to be the feudal overlord of the Shang heartland around Anyang. This served a double purpose: it kept the former Shang subjects pacified under a ruler of the accustomed family, and it assured that the sacrifices to the Shang ancestors would continue properly. The Chou king had no wish to offend that long line of grim spirits.

However, he knew that it was risky to leave a Shang prince in a position of power. King Wu appointed two of his own younger brothers, Kuan Shu and Ts'ai Shu, to "aid" the Shang scion. This cautious arrangement backfired, though; the Shang prince was able to wean the two Chou princes away from their brother and win their support in a revolt that would re-establish Shang supremacy.

At this point, several years after the conquest, King Wu died. His son and heir, Ch'eng, was too young to rule. Power was assumed by another of the late king's brothers, the Duke of Chou, an extraordinary individual given many miraculous powers by the annalists. The forceful regent quelled the Shang uprising, putting to death the Shang ruler and one of his own two rebellious brothers, exiling the other. To prevent a renewal of Shang spirit, the great Shang capital was totally destroyed and its people transported to the remote district of Sung. The Shang homeland was repopulated with loyal subjects and given as a fief to another royal Chou brother, who took the title of Marquis of Wei. Then, to the amazement of everyone, the Duke of Chou resigned his regency when the rightful heir came of age and placed King Ch'eng in full control.

The remnants of the Shang people were permitted to have a Shang ruler. He was Wei Tzŭ, a brother of the last reigning Shang king, who had quarreled with him and gone into exile. Evidently it was thought that he could be trusted to remain loyal, unlike the previous Shang puppet ruler. The Duke of Chou felt it necessary to take the risk, because the sacrifices to the departed Shang monarchs had to be continued by a man of their line.

During the centuries that followed, the Chou Dynasty established itself, flourished, built great cities, unsuccessfully imitated the Shang bronzes, and sponsored a marvelous flowering of Chinese literature and philosophy. Eventually the feudal dukes of the various states grew too powerful and the center failed to hold, so that after 771 B.C. the Chou ruler was little more than a figurehead and contending states vied for authority, creating a long period of chaos and warfare that ended only with the unification of China under the Ch'in Dynasty in 221 B.C.

During the eight centuries of the Chou period, the small state of Sung clung to a precarious existence, carrying on the rites of the glorious Shang past. We can picture the Sung rulers—not to be confused with the unrelated Sung Dynasty founded in A.D. 960—as a somewhat seedy aristocracy, living in shadowed halls and brooding on past splendors, looking askance at the rude barbarians who now held real authority. This is the impression that is derived from an incident of 638 B.C., when Sung was invaded by troops of the state of Ch'u. The men of Sung armed themselves quickly and came upon the invaders in a state of disarray, crossing a river. The Sung minister of war said to the Duke of Sung, "They are many and we are few. Pray let us attack them before they have all crossed over."

"It may not be done," the Duke of Sung replied.

After the Ch'u soldiers had crossed the river, but before they had assembled for battle, the minister again asked permission to attack. "Not yet," replied the Duke. He waited until the enemy was in full readiness. Then the battle was joined, and Sung was badly beaten, the Duke himself suffering a severe wound. When his people remonstrated with him for failing to take advantage of his opportunity, he replied with quiet dignity, "The superior man does not inflict a second wound, or take the gray-haired prisoner. When the ancients had their armies in the field, they would not attack an enemy when he was in a defile. Though I am but the unworthy remnant of a fallen dynasty, I would not sound my drums to attack an unprepared enemy."

The tone is perfect: the aristocrat come upon evil times, haughtily refusing to lower himself to the unchivalrous modern level. And so Sung remained, the last outpost of Shang greatness, until a time came when China fell under one rule and was shackled by the Great Wall of Emperor Ch'in Shih Huang Ti. By then, Shang and Chou alike were only dusty memories, names out of a dark past.

The name of Chou remained alive, because of the multitudinous documents set down under that dynasty. Shang passed into legend and dwelt in the realm of myth for hundreds of years—until the archeologists came to Anyang and restored to reality this cruel, enigmatic, wholly fascinating line of fearless warriors and matchless craftsmen.

Four

Zimbabwe: City Of Stone

BEFORE THE WHITE MAN came to Africa and made it a continent for plunder, black kingdoms and empires of great might and complexity held sway there. These nations of medieval Africa left no written archives, so our record of their existence comes mainly from tribal traditions, blurred and distorted, and from the accounts set down by Arab and Portuguese traders who visited them while they still endured. We know the names of a few of these lost empires: Ghana, Mali, Benin, Songhai. Some of these names once again mark the African map, now that newly independent states, reaching backward to their legendary past, replace the conqueror's detested labels for their lands.

Sometimes the evidence is more concrete than that of tradition and chronicle. In the remote back country of Southern Rhodesia lie the ruins of Great Zimbabwe, an incredible city of stone. Zimbabwe stands as mute testimony to the might of a vanished empire and contradicts the arguments of those who claim that black Africans could build nothing sturdier than huts of mud. Zimbabwe remains and someday may again lend its name to a Negro nation. Just as Northern Rhodesia has become Zambia now that Africans rule it once more, Southern Rhodesia is called Zimbabwe by the black nationalists locked in the struggle for independence, and the strange, ghost-haunted fortress of stone is the symbol of that struggle.

Zimbabwe is a native word meaning "stone houses." It was applied centuries ago not only to the stone city of that name but to the black kingdom whose capital that city was. Zimbabwe was still alive and flourishing when the Portuguese arrived early in the sixteenth century, following in the wake of Vasco da Gama. Once Vasco had shown the way around the Cape of Good Hope, the Portuguese established themselves as merchants along the southeast coast of Africa, to the annoyance of the Arabs who had long monopolized trade in those parts.

Gold, of course, interested the Portuguese more than anything else. In their coastal strongholds they heard rumors of a great inland kingdom where gold was mined, but they did not dare venture toward the interior for fear of being cut down by marauding tribesmen. Diogo de Alcançova, reporting from Africa to the King of Portugal in 1506, whetted his greed with talk of a gold-mining land called Vealanga and a city known as Zumubany, as his Portuguese ears heard *Zimbabwe* pronounced:

And, Sir, a man might go from Sofala to a city which is called Zumubany, which is large, in which the king always resides, in ten or twelve days, if you travel as in Portugal; but because they do not travel except from morning until midday, and eat and sleep until the next morning when they go on again, they cannot go to this city in less than twenty or twenty-four days; and in the whole kingdom of Vealanga gold is extracted; and in this way: they dig out the earth and make a kind of tunnel, through which they go under the ground a long stone's throw, and keep on taking out from the veins with the ground mixed with the gold, and, when collected, they put it in a pot, and cook it much in fire; and after cooking they take it out, and put it to cool, and, when cold, the earth remains, and the gold all fine gold . . . and no man can take it out without leave from the king, under penalty of death.

Eleven years later, Duarte Barbosa, another Portuguese adventurer, had a further report on this kingdom and a new spelling for its capital. He told of the black men "clad in the skins of wild beasts" who carried "swords thrust into wooden scabbards bound with much gold and other metals" and were armed with spears and bows as well. "The iron arrowheads are long and finely pointed," he related. "They are warlike men, and some too are great traders."

Barbosa told his king that "fifteen or twenty days' journey inland is a great town called Zimbaoche, in which are many houses of wood and of straw." From a contemporary of Barbosa's named de Goes came the information that this city contained "a fortress built of large and heavy stones inside and out . . . a very curious and well-constructed building, as according to report no lime to join the stones can be seen." João de Barros, a Portuguese geographer summing up available knowledge a generation later, declared that the wall of this fortress was "more than twenty-five spans in width" and spoke of a nearby tower "more than twelve fathoms high."

If the Portuguese ever beheld Zimbabwe with their own eyes, we have no record of it. All accounts are secondhand, and some are full of errors, like that of de Barros, who writes of a nonexistent square fortress and of unknown inscriptions above the doors. The stone buildings, states de Barros, were called "Symbaoe" by the natives, "which according to their language signifies court." That is, he meant, they were royal property. "When, and by whom, these edifices were raised, as the people of the land are ignorant of the art of writing, there is no record, but they say they are the work of the devil, for in comparison with their power and knowledge it does not seem possible to them that they should be the work of man."

The Portuguese foothold along the coast proved to be a sturdy one, as the continued presence of their colony of Mozambique today indicates. But Zimbabwe, lying west of Mozambique's inland frontier, apparently was beyond their reach and remained in native hands. No Europeans came to it, only Africans and Arab traders, to whom it was nothing remarkable, simply a stone city in the middle of nowhere.

Not until the nineteenth century did Europeans again become aware of Zimbabwe, 450 years after the Portuguese traders first sent word home about it. Adam Render, a hunter who had deserted his family to live among the tribesmen of Matabeleland in what is now the Republic of South Africa, saw Zimbabwe in 1868, though he did not record his impressions of it. About the same time, a German schoolteacher named Karl Gottlieb Mauch was legging it through Africa, and Mauch put Zimbabwe on the map.

He was an odd sort, with huge shoulders and a flowing beard, tramping across the wastelands in an antelope skin suit and hobnailed boots. Born in 1837, he was swept up by the fascination for Africa, and before he turned twenty-eight he was landing at Durban to explore the unknown region south of the Zambezi River. He was self-educated and self-propelled and traveled alone, on foot, with a sixty-pound pack on his back. "I could at least hope," he wrote,

that my things would suffer less damage than if I had entrusted them to careless or frequently destructive bearers. For my books (which did not include any "light reading") I transformed a small waterproof gun-case into a kind of satchel which could be suspended from some part of my anatomy. Besides those volumes which would be used several times during the day, this held an almanac, a table of logarithms, a book on botany and a treatise on minerals; mathematical instruments, paintbox, diaries, sketchbook, writing materials, and a towel, brush and comb.

Equipped also with pliers, awls, whetstone, a sewing kit, medicines, a compass, a sextant, two revolvers, an umbrella, a double-barreled gun, and a variety of other useful objects, Mauch hiked through the Transvaal, a hot dry district sparsely settled by tight-lipped, God-fearing Boer farmers. When his shoe soles wore thin, he replaced them with giraffe hide. When hunger troubled him, he foraged in hollow trees for supplies of honey. An elephant hunter named Hartley taught him about game, recommending hippopotamus bacon enthusiastically and suggesting that he avoid eating crocodile meat or ostrich flesh.

Hartley took him into desert country, where Mauch proceeded to strike gold wherever he pulled up stones for examination. The geology textbooks he carried told him that he stood above a potential fortune. But rampaging Matabele tribesmen made the neighborhood unsafe, and Mauch moved on, leaving others to make the fabulous gold hauls of a generation later. He had come to Africa, he said, to explore, not to grow rich.

His explorations led him northward toward the Zambezi. But he fell into the hands of a local chief who imprisoned him for six months and parted him from most of his possessions. Penniless now, fever-smitten, the undeterred Mauch regained his freedom and in the summer of 1871 made his way toward the mysterious inland ruins of Zimbabwe, which Adam Render had found three years earlier.

Living on roots and beans, fending off the attacks of the natives, Mauch proceeded northward until he was within a dozen miles of Zimbabwe. Then he was captured by another chief, but Adam Render himself arrived providentially to set him free; Render had married a Matabele princess, and the natives respected him. With Render's help, Mauch headed for the ruins. On the evening of September 5, 1871, he clambered up a hill and found himself beholding Zimbabwe's majestic masonry.

For days he explored and mapped the maze of buildings. Then, as though supplied by a tour office, an aged native named Babareke appeared. He was, he said, the son of the last "high priest" of Zimbabwe. Marauders had slain his father and carried off the sacrificial vessels long ago, and the old man did not know how to perform the ancient rites. He offered his son as a guide to accompany Mauch to the German's home. "There," the old man said, "he will learn from your priest how to offer the right sort of sacrifice to the god. I am too old and my fate is uncertain."

Mauch could supply no information about Zimbabwe's former rituals, but he accepted the native guide. The following May he set out on foot for Mozambique, 563 miles away. After an exhausting journey, they reached the city of Sena, where Mauch parted from his companion and boarded a riverboat bound down the Zambezi to the coast. Tattered and worn, Mauch wangled passage back to Europe, where he died a few years later when he fell from the window of his house.

Before his death, though, Mauch published a description of Zimbabwe and offered some speculative thoughts on the identity of its builders, thereby spawning a theory that remained stubbornly persistent for decades and still has its supporters.

Mauch found it impossible to believe that the backward, nearly naked tribesmen of Matabeleland could have constructed anything so impressive as the stone buildings of Zimbabwe. How could mere ignorant blacks have been such master architects? No, Zimbabwe must be the work of some high civilization of antiquity. And Mauch knew which one. Zimbabwe was none other than the Biblical land of Ophir, and its builders were Phoenician colonists or perhaps the subjects of the Queen of Sheba, the Sabaeans.

The Old Testament tells how King Solomon hired the Phoenician navy of King Hiram of Tyre to bring gold from Ophir. Jehoshaphat, King of Judah, also is described as using "ships of Tharshish to go to Ophir for gold: but they went not; for the ships were broken at Ezion-geber." Just where Ophir was located has long been a matter for scholarly debate. Some authorities have placed it in south Arabia, others in India. Mauch put it in eastern Africa and identified the hilltop fortress of Zimbabwe as a copy of Solomon's temple on Mount Moriah. An elliptical building of great size in the valley below was surely a replica of the place in which the Queen of Sheba had stayed while visiting Jerusalem in the tenth century B.C., he said.

Other adventurers came to Mauch's "land of Ophir" to ransack the ruins for gold. One, a South African trader named Willi Posselt, arrived at Zimbabwe in 1888, finding no gold but several large beams of soft stone, five feet long and a few inches thick, whose upper ends were carved with the images of hawklike birds. Posselt saw that there might be cash value in such an artifact, so he hacked the image from one beam and carried it away. Entering the conical tower within the main enclosure, Posselt found its interior "covered with dense bush: tall trees towered above the undergrowth, and suspended from them were masses of 'monkey rope,' by means of which we lowered ourselves and entered the ruins. I could not find any trace of human remains or of any implements, nor was the hope of discovering any treasure rewarded with success."

Posselt observed that "profound silence brooded over the scene." That silence was broken often in the next decade. The empire builder Cecil Rhodes bought Posselt's "Zimbabwe Bird" and grew so interested that he sent Theodore Bent, a veteran traveler and antiquary, to explore Zimbabwe in 1891. Bent visited the ruins with his wife and a surveyor named R. M. Swan. The following year Bent's book, *Ruined Cities of Mashonaland,* appeared, going into several editions almost at once and stirring widespread interest. Bent, too, believed that Zimbabwe was the work of white-skinned (or at least no more than swarthy)

Phoenicians or Sabaeans, and that the gold mines surrounding the ruins were in fact the fabled mines of Ophir.

It was difficult for Englishmen to believe otherwise in 1892. There was much talk of "the white man's burden," and the inferiority of the black races was taken so much for granted that no one seriously questioned the point. Though the English tried to be kindly to "natives," they did not hesitate to apply *force majeure* to any tribes that gave trouble. They were only savages. Everyone knew that the only true builders and shapers of civilization were the whites.

Here were the Zimbabwe ruins, now: sixty acres of stone buildings with high walls carefully fashioned from flat slabs of granite. Atop a 350-foot hill nicknamed "the Acropolis" rose a sturdy tower, and in the plain below sprawled a complex mass of buildings dominated by an elliptical one, some three hundred feet across, known as "the Temple." The walls of the Temple stood thirty feet high in some places and reached thicknesses of fourteen feet. Inner walls divided the enclosure into areas joined by passageways, and within the heart of the structure stood a stone tower, cone-shaped, fifty feet in circumference at the base, thirty-two feet to its shattered summit. Such buildings the works of blacks? Could natives have devised the elegant herringbone and chevron patterns of the masonry? It was as reasonable to think that the whole city had been built by diligent chimpanzees.

An archeologist named Sir John Willoughby came to Zimbabwe in 1892 to extend Bent's findings. He damaged the ruins considerably as he burrowed through them, but at least his intentions were honorably scientific. Not so honorable were the aims of the Ancient Ruins Company, Ltd., chartered in Johannesburg in 1894 to "exploit all the ancient ruins south of the Zambesi." Its founders, a prospector named Neal and two investors named Clark and Gifford, visited some forty-three ruins in the next five years. "We have got some 25 ounces of Gold and the manufacture of jewellery is even finer than the other lot," Neal informed his backers in 1895. "Old George dropped on to two of their hiding places and got about 6 lb. weight in one and 3 lb. in the other." These entrepreneurs collected about five hundred ounces of gold through such activities, some of it raw ore, some of it in the form of worked pieces that were melted down for their metallic value. Where the walls of ancient buildings barred their progress, they simply hacked them apart.

By 1900, the damage these treasure seekers were doing had come to the attention of Cecil Rhodes, and he shut the company down. A belated antiquities law, passed in 1902, made further enterprises of this kind illegal in Rhodesia. Prospector Neal turned into archeologist Neal and collaborated with a local journalist named Richard Hall on a volume titled *Ancient Ruins of Rhodesia,* which once more set forth the Phoenician-Sabaean theory of Zimbabwe's origin. The book appeared in 1902 and received such acclaim that Hall won appointment as official curator of the Zimbabwe ruins. He began trenching with alacrity, observing what he imagined to be the contemporary rules of scientific excavation. Gouging his way through the Zimbabwe deposits, Hall scrambled the stratification in horrifying manner and proudly reported on his endeavors in his book of 1905, *Great Zimbabwe.*

Hall emerged as the most vociferous member of the Phoenician-Sabaean school. He identified two main periods of construction at Zimbabwe: a Sabaean phase, from 2000 to 1000 B.C., and a Phoenician phase, "somewhat anterior to 1100 B.C., down to some time before the Christian era." From Zimbabwe had come the gold of Ophir; and, naturally, its builders had been white men looked upon with awe by the ignorant black natives.

The first man who seriously challenged this assumption was a young British archeologist named David Randall-MacIver. Randall-MacIver, a protégé of the great Sir Flinders Petrie, was chosen in 1905 by the British Association for the Advancement of Science to make a fresh study of the Rhodesian ruins. He reported on his study of seven sites, including Zimbabwe, in his book of 1906, *Medieval Rhodesia.* Randall-MacIver's findings wholly differed from those of Zimbabwe's previous explorers. The ruins, he said, were purely African in origin. They had been built by black men, and relatively recently, too: he had found no object "which can be shown to be more ancient than the fourteenth or fifteenth centuries."

In a direct and often vitriolic attack on Hall, Randall-MacIver insisted that "the arts and manufactures exemplified by objects found within the dwellings are typically African, except when the objects are imports of well-known medieval or post-medieval date." He saw "not a trace of Oriental or European style of any period whatever." He deplored the underlying racial prejudices that seemed to have shaped the conclusions of earlier archeologists at Zimbabwe.

Hall, stung by the charges, replied in 1909 with *Prehistoric Rhodesia,* which provoked further response from Randall-MacIver. They battled for some twenty years, until the dispute over the origins of Zimbabwe took on the aspect of a personal, highly emotional feud. White supremacists lined up behind Hall, and partisans of African culture behind Randall-MacIver. The controversy was explosive and far removed from a scientific level.

In 1929 the British Association sent another expedition to Zimbabwe with the hope of clarifying the situation. It was headed by Dr. Gertrude Caton-Thompson, and among its members was the youthful Kathleen Kenyon, her Jericho fame still a quarter of a century in the future.

Miss Caton-Thompson's report, *The Zimbabwe Culture* (1931) was generally a vindication of Randall-MacIver. She was unable to detect any evidence disproving the African origin and medieval date of Zimbabwe and declared that she could not "fall in with the oft-repeated and compromising suggestion that Zimbabwe and its allied structures were built by native workmen under the direction of a 'superior' alien race or supervisor." She admitted the possibility of foreign influence, a trace of Islamic mosque design in the conical tower, perhaps an Arabic flavor to the chevron designs in the masonry, but to her these did not seem to detract from the accomplishment of the black builders.

The matter did not rest there. The German ethnologist Leo Frobenius, a respected figure though not an archeologist, also published a book on Zimbabwe in 1931. He supported the Mauch-Hall theory of a non-African origin. Though most archeologists were willing to accept Miss Caton-Thompson's conclusions, supported as they were by elegant stratigraphic surveys, Frobenius' viewpoint won backers in many quarters. The "myth" of Zimbabwe's origin seemed romantic and alluring to those who wished to enjoy fantasies of a lost white colony in prehistoric Rhodesia. Such novels as H. Rider Haggard's *King Solomon's Mines* helped to shape the popular impression of Zimbabwe's great age and non-African genesis.

Alas for the romantics, the thrilling tales of Phoenician cities in Black Africa could not withstand the cold light of scientific examination. The Southern Rhodesian Monuments Commission inaugurated a general survey of the local archeological sites in 1938, though the war interrupted the work before Zimbabwe could be studied. By the time the project was resumed, in 1958, the excavators had the benefit of such modern archeological advances as carbon-14 dating. In collaboration with the National Museum of Southern Rhodesia, the Monuments Commission reopened Miss Caton-Thompson's trenches under the direction of Roger Summers, the National Museum's curator. The Summers expedition offered for the first time a detailed account of the ebb and flow of African civilization at the Zimbabwe site over the past two thousand years.

Interestingly, Summers found kind words for Richard Hall, the most dogged of the now-discredited Phoenician-Sabaean school. Though he could not accept Hall's conclusions, Summers observed that there was "somewhat more value in Hall's book than was at one time apparent. Despite the piling of fancy on fact, it now seems that when Hall reports facts only, he is a reliable witness." Summers showed that one of the most bitter points of disagreement between Hall and Randall-MacIver, the interpretation of an enclosure in the great Temple, had arisen from a failure of communication: each man had been talking about a different section of the enclosure.

What they saw, they honestly and correctly reported. As they were not on the spot together, neither realized the exact section the other was describing, and so charges of unsound excavation technique were countered by allegations of intellectual chicanery and the whole issue completely clouded. The tragedy is not that they were both right but that the bitterness of the quarrel completely misled everybody.

Roger Summers drew his own synthesis of the Zimbabwe story from many sources. The basic text, of course, was the record in the earth, his own excavation findings, carefully documented and where possible tagged with a carbon-14 date. But he also made use of the Portuguese and Arabic accounts of the medieval black kingdoms of Rhodesia and of the oral traditions of the modern-day inhabitants of the region. No one had troubled to question the natives about Zimbabwe before 1941, when the German ethnologist Heinrich Wieschhoff finally collected a body of local tradition which, though scanty, was important and revealing. Summers pursued this approach with substantial results. As an African chief told a member of Summers' party in 1961, "If only you white people had asked the old people about Zimbabwe when you first came to the country, we'd all know a lot more about it now."

At the time King Solomon was sending ships to bring back the gold of Ophir, the site of Zimbabwe was occupied by Neolithic tribesmen of the Bushman racial stock. These nomadic hunters left crude paintings on the hill of Zimbabwe, and skeletons of their distinctive type were found in the early levels of occupation there.

A new, racially different people came into the area about A.D. 100, probably from the north. These were taller people of a more advanced culture, who knew the use of metals and who made pottery. The arrival of the newcomers marks the beginning of the Iron Age at Zimbabwe. Thick deposits of their pottery were found by the Caton-Thompson expedition of 1929. Summers' carbon-14 studies showed that the manufacture of this type of pottery ceased in the third or fourth century A.D.

What brought these Iron Age folk to the Zimbabwe region was the lure of gold. Few gold mines have been discovered at Zimbabwe itself, but the stone city lies in the center of a vast gold field: more than 60,000 ancient mines have been recorded.

The gold was easy to get. In many places it simply lay in gleaming nuggets on the surface, exposed by erosion. Though this source must have dried up in time, it was no real challenge to mine the metal, for it was found in rich vertical "reefs" thrusting down between veins of quartz and other hard rock. The miners simply followed the reefs down as far as they could go, breaking the ore loose with stone wedges or with iron points fixed in wooden shafts and driven home with hammers of stone. Where the quartz intruded to block the downward progress, the miners built small fires, dousing them quickly with water to crack the stone.

The Iron Age people avoided horizontal reefs, for they had no capability for shoring up the roof of a shaft with timbers to prevent accidents. They were content to mine vertically, usually descending twenty-five to forty feet, though some of their shafts went down more than a hundred feet. Such deep shafts were astonishingly narrow, and the miners who worked them were slender girls barely five feet tall. Some of them were trapped in the shafts, and their skeletons told the tale for later archeologists.

Such victims of mine catastrophes provided another bit of information: they showed that the Bushmen and the new Iron Age folk continued to live side by side at Zimbabwe during this phase. Bushman skeletons are common in the shafts. We do not know, of course, whether these simpler people learned the techniques of mining from the newcomers or whether they were enslaved by the intruders and forced to work the mines.

The great stone city at Zimbabwe was still unbuilt during this early gold-mining period. Iron Age craftsmanship was shown instead by the pottery, a ware decorated with lines and incised dots on a red background. By A.D. 400 the makers of this handsome pottery were no longer occupying Zimbabwe, and it seems that the site remained abandoned for hundreds of years thereafter.

The next level of occupation dates from about A.D. 1000, according to Summers. New migrants filtered into Rhodesia, makers of plain black pottery less attractive than the earlier red ware. These people were cattle raisers, for they left small clay models of their beasts. They decked themselves in wound wire ornaments of bronze and used a variety of iron tools.

Several successive waves of these people entered the region. And sometime in the eleventh or twelfth century, the first great stone walls were built at Zimbabwe.

The carbon-14 dates for the first walls involve some minor mysteries. Summers found that the wall-building phase began in

A.D. 1085, with a margin of error of 120 years either way. (Such margins of error are common features of all carbon-14 calculations.) But fragments of drainage timber taken from the base of one of the walls of the elliptical building in the valley produced carbon-14 dates of A.D. 591 ± 120 years and A.D. 702 ± 92 years. Which set of dates was correct—those found in most of the wall deposits, or the two strangely early ones from the elliptical building?

Summers clung to the eleventh-century date for the beginning of the wall-building phase. The earlier dates could be explained in several ways, not even taking into account the possibility of an error in the reading. The wall builders might have re-used logs that had been cut several centuries before for earlier constructions. Or they could have employed the wood of dead trees whose carbon-14 intake had ceased hundreds of years earlier.

The first stone structures of Zimbabwe were built with steep vertical walls, thin in relation to their height, made of untrimmed stones of varying sizes. No mortar was used, and the walls rose flush from the ground without foundations. The wall of the Acropolis, rising above a sheer cliff face ninety feet high, is an example of this style of architecture. Another is a wall northwest of the Temple, which unfortunately was largely ruined by Sir John Willoughby during his 1893 excavations.

Willoughby's work, though it wreaked havoc with Zimbabwe, produced a useful dating clue to corroborate the carbon-14 findings. Digging in the building with the earliest wall, Willoughby uncovered what he called "pieces of sea-green china." Similar porcelain potsherds have been found at other Rhodesian sites, and they have been identified as Celadon ware from Sung Dynasty China, with a twelfth- or thirteenth-century date. This export ware may have found its way via Arab traders to the Rhodesian interior about A.D. 1300, which supplies a date for the first-phase buildings of Zimbabwe.

Who were the builders?

On the basis of the pottery found in these levels—a plain, rough ware decorated with crosshatched bands—Summers has tentatively suggested that the builders were of the Shona group, Shona being a language still in use along Africa's southeastern coast. There is linguistic evidence indicating that Shona has been spoken in the area for about a thousand years, and the Shona-speaking peoples of the present day continue to make a pottery similar to the Zimbabwe ware of A.D. 1300. The Shona of Southern Rhodesia today also retain a skill for building with stone which they may well have inherited from the first architects of Zimbabwe.

During the fifteenth century, there were small but significant changes at Zimbabwe. Pottery styles altered, and so did the techniques of architecture. The new buildings (given a carbon-14 date of A.D. 1450 ± 150) used carefully trimmed stones of nearly uniform size, rising with startling regularity from foundation trenches. Most of the surviving structures at Zimbabwe are of this type, though they appear to have been built over a span of several centuries.

The evidence indicates that one Negro empire had replaced another—with Zimbabwe, the capital, undergoing a large-scale reconstruction.

The earlier of these realms was that of the Monomotapa, a Shona-speaking stock who may have been the first builders of Zimbabwe. *Monomotapa* evidently was the title of the ruler of this state, and the Arabs extended it to refer to the state itself. The Monomotapa arose around the twelfth century and seemingly remained in possession of Zimbabwe for some 250 years. They conquered outlying districts and established a feudal domain. This, however, was riddled with internal dissension and intrigue, and the problem of maintaining communication throughout Monomotapa territory became insuperable.

When the Portuguese arrived at the beginning of the sixteenth century, the Monomotapa had already passed the peak of their glory. Under a chief named Matope, they had expanded their reign over a vast region running from the interior to the Indian Ocean. But after Matope's death in 1480, a secessionist movement began in the isolated southern provinces of the Monomotapa empire. Its leader was Changa, the head of a Shona-speaking tribe called the Rozwi. Encouraged by the Arab merchants of the coast, Changa proclaimed Rozwi independence upon Matope's death. The new Monomotapa monarch, Nyahuma, attempted to quell Changa's secession and was himself slain in battle by Changa in 1490. For four years, Changa ruled the entire empire, until he was assassinated by a member of the old Monomotapa royal family.

By 1500, the situation had reached some stability: the Monomotapa ruled over what is now the northern half of Southern Rhodesia and an adjoining strip 600 miles long and 100 to 200 miles wide running southeast to the coast. This left Zimbabwe in their possession. The Rozwi, ruled by the descendants of Changa, controlled what had been the southern and eastern provinces of the Monomotapa empire. The Portuguese, when they appeared a few years later, established good relations with the Monomotapa but were unable to make much headway with the belligerent Rozwi of the south. While the Portuguese were gradually turning the Monomotapa into cooperative subjects, the Rozwi remained fiercely independent and continued to hatch imperialistic designs against the territory of their neighbors.

Zimbabwe may have changed hands several times between 1450 and 1600, during the struggle between these two Shona-speaking realms. That would explain the presence of some buildings of the newer Rozwi style among the Monomotapa structures. But not until the late sixteenth century did the Rozwi at last make themselves the permanent masters of Zimbabwe.

Under a dynasty of kings who called themselves the Mambos, the Rozwi hammered at the Monomotapa. By 1700 the Monomotapa state was destroyed, and more than a million Africans were under the rule of the Rozwi Mambos. Their empire extended over some 240,000 square miles, from the Zambezi River in the north to the mountains of Transvaal in the south, from the Indian Ocean to the parched dreariness of Bechuanaland. Zimbabwe lay roughly in the heart of this huge domain. For five or six centuries, various Shona-speaking tribes had erected stone structures there, but now Zimbabwe came into its greatest period of expansion.

The Rozwi may have been aided in the construction work by another tribe, the Mwenye, who lacked political ambitions and were famed for their craftsmanship. Roger Summers found that both the Rozwi and the Mwenye of today have tribal traditions of being "the builders of Zimbabwe." Since there is little doubt that the Rozwi were the rulers of Zimbabwe from the end of the seventeenth century on, it is possible that the Mwenye served as construction workers at the bidding of the more aggressive tribe.

The building material was granite, as it had been from the start at Zimbabwe. The workmen split the flat slabs away from the cliffs by heating the rock and pouring water into crevices. Timber beams were used to pry the cracked slabs loose. Since the natives had no wheeled vehicles, they had to haul the stone from the quarries to Zimbabwe on sledges. The trimming of the stone was done at the construction site. The main area of building during this period was in the valley rather than on the hilltop. The features known as the Conical Tower, the Great Outer Wall, and the Temple were built at this time.

Roger Summers felt that the wall, one of Zimbabwe's most spectacular achievements, was built in a clockwise direction starting just west of the main entrance to the entire complex, and that the workmen used the rising wall as a ramp up which they carried stone for the upper reaches. A change in the slope of the wall halfway up suggests that it was built in two stages, or that two teams of builders were at work.

"One visualizes," writes Summers,

an architect controlling two or perhaps four teams of builders erecting the inner and outer faces simultaneously; there would be very few actual builders but there would be a veritable army of trimmers, carriers, sledge drivers, quarrymen, wood collectors and water bearers to keep the builders supplied, and the organization of this immense gang, totalling perhaps two or three hundred men and women, would call for administrative qualities of no mean order—qualities which tradition says were possessed by the Rozwi.

Gold was the basis of Rozwi prosperity. The Rhodesian gold mines, which had been worked since the coming of the Iron Age people about A.D. 100, still yielded a shining harvest. In those early days, the gold had been mined for the simplest of reasons: it was fine gleaming stuff that made attractive ornaments. But now the Rozwi found a more sophisticated use for the yellow metal: they carried it to the coastal towns and traded it to the

Arabs and Portuguese for other goods. The Portuguese chose to stamp it into little disks instead of making jewelry from it, but that was their business. The Rozwi were good bargainers, and they got a stiff price for their gold. The deposits at Zimbabwe contain blue-and-white Ming Dynasty porcelain from Nanking, beads from India, Europe, and Indonesia, metal implements from European foundries, and glass bottles that once had held good Dutch gin.

Not all the Rozwi gold went to the export trade, though. They kept back part of their supply to fashion into beads and bracelets. These golden trinkets must have been liberally scattered through the surface layers of the Zimbabwe deposits when Mauch visited the place in 1871. But the treasure seekers who dug at Zimbabwe in the closing years of the nineteenth century carried off huge quantities of gold: wire, chain, foil, beads weighing as much as an ounce apiece, even nails and tacks. The infamous Ancient Ruins Company, melting these things down to sell by weight, shortsightedly deprived itself of even greater profits by failing to see their value as artifacts. And Richard Hall, a treasure hunter with some pretensions as an archeologist, admitted to have found $20,000 worth of gold in three years' digging at Zimbabwe—again, calculating by the metallic value alone.

The wealth of golden objects that these plunderers carried off was suggested by the discovery in 1932 of another Rozwi site two hundred miles to the southwest at Mapungubwe. No Ancient Ruins Company managed to loot Mapungubwe. It had long been regarded by the natives as "a place of fear," and they had refused to climb it or even to discuss it with whites. The Boer farmers of the district had heard rumors, though, of a "sacred hill' studded with buried treasure, and they frequently pressed the natives for information about it.

At length a farmer named van Graan coaxed a reluctant African into telling him that Mapungubwe was the sacred hill. The native showed van Graan a way to scale the hill, which was about one hundred feet high and one thousand feet long. Accompanied by his son and three other men, the farmer hacked his way through the thorny underbrush until a clearing emerged. They found themselves at the foot of a rock face into which small holes had been cut, as if for the rungs of a ladder. Scrambling up this steep incline to the summit, the five Boers saw a low stone fortification and an array of large, well-balanced boulders set out as though to be tipped down on any attackers.

Potsherds, beads, and bits of iron and copper littered the hilltop. In one place a heavy rain had opened a breach in the soil, and van Graan spied the welcome gleam of gold. According to Dr. Fouché of the University of Pretoria, who carried on excavations there several years later, "An excited search now started, and soon the members of the party were finding gold beads, bangles, and bits of thin gold plating." It was the last day of 1932, and the five men saw the old year out gleefully. They continued their search the following morning, scratching through the loose soil with their knives. Fouché tells us:

They found large pieces of plate gold, some of them shaped. These were the remains of little rhinoceroses which had consisted of thin plate gold tacked by means of little gold tacks on to some core of wood or other substance which had perished. Solid gold tails and ears, beautifully made, had likewise been tacked on to these figures. Presently they came upon the remains of a skeleton, which was dug out carefully; but the skull and most of the bones crumbled to dust on being exposed to the air.

These preliminary explorations produced nearly five pounds of gold—several thousand dollars' worth, at the metal value alone. Obviously the hill held much more. But the consciences of the discoverers were troubled. Van Graan's son had studied at Pretoria, a pupil of Fouché, and after some debate he shipped a few specimens of the gold to his former teacher.

The archeological importance of the discovery was easily apparent. Here was an untouched treasure-trove of elegant wrought-gold objects, possibly a major site related to the Zimbabwe culture. Professor van Riet Lowe of the University of Pretoria set out at once for Mapungubwe to inspect the deposits, and the van Graans and their three companions turned over all the objects they had taken. When Dr. Lowe reported that the hilltop must certainly have been a significant outpost of prehistoric African culture and was intact but for the surface diggings of the van Graan party, the University promptly acquired the site.

From 1934 and 1939 Fouché led excavations at Mapungubwe. He discovered stone structures of the Zimbabwe type and a remarkable horde of gold. In the 1934 season, an archeologist stumbled upon a "royal burial ground" containing twenty-three skeletons bedecked with gold. One skeleton alone had been buried with more than seventy ounces of golden baubles, while another's legs were festooned with over a hundred circlets of coiled gold wire. Some twelve thousand golden beads were recovered from the site.

Fouché published a preliminary report in 1937, but further information on Mapungubwe remained in manuscript form until 1955. By then, carbon-14 analysis showed that the hill had been occupied prior to the eleventh century, and that the Rozwi had begun to build there in the fourteenth. It represents a kind of early version of Great Zimbabwe—and Mapungubwe's lavish golden treasures, all of them safely recovered and preserved in museums, tell us what sort of El Dorado fell to the Ancient Ruins Company and associated looters at Zimbabwe in the 1890's.

During its summit of grandeur in the eighteenth century, Zimbabwe must have been a bustling metropolis, thronged by a proud African nobility ornamented in brilliant arrays of golden splendor. It was the political capital of the Rozwi empire, but it also was a holy city: Jerusalem combined with the District of Columbia. Here dwelt the Rozwi Mambo, all but inaccessible in his high-walled palace, surrounded by the clustering houses of his courtiers. And atop the hill was the sacred place of the Rozwi, where solemn rain-making rituals were performed.

Karl Gottleib Mauch provided the first clue to this, when he told of encountering the son of the last Rozwi priest, a pathetic aged man who had forgotten the ancient rituals. Modern ethnologists, questioning the natives, have learned that the ceremonies once performed atop the hill of Zimbabwe still are carried on in cave shrines elsewhere in the country. One of these shrines is close to the stone buildings of Zimbabwe, and Summers observes that an African headman referred to this shrine as "the real Zimbabwe."

The handsome pillars of stone, topped with the carved figures of hawklike birds, originally stood in the most holy part of the hilltop sanctuary. Eight of these are known today. One, the hacked-off bird that Willi Posselt sold to Cecil Rhodes in 1890, is now an ornament of the official residence of South Africa's prime minister. Five are in the South African Museum in Capetown, brought there by Theodore Bent after he found them in 1891. One is in the National Museum of Rhodesia at Bulawayo, and the eighth is in two pieces thousands of miles apart, with a fragment in the Queen Victoria Museum, Salisbury, Rhodesia, and another in an East Berlin museum.

The construction of Great Zimbabwe continued all through this flourishing era. While the Thirteen Colonies were breaking free from England's grip, black architects were raising ever-higher walls on that Rhodesian hilltop for the greater glory of their Mambo. While King George III reigned, the Mambo Dimbeywu moved about his domain from city to stone city. Heads fell and blood flowed in Parisian streets as new enclosures were added to the maze in Zimbabwe's valley.

The end came with frightening swiftness for this great empire, which had crushed the Monomotapa and outsmarted the Portuguese. In the part of southeastern Africa that Europeans called Natal, a tribe known as the Zulu had become fearsome warriors under a chief named Dingiswayo, who came to power in 1807. Dingiswayo's successor was the brilliant madman and inspired general, Shaka, whose atrocious cruelties stained much of South Africa with the gore of his foes. Those tribes that Shaka either could not or would not absorb into his own state, he systematically massacred.

This produced a steady flow of refugees, trekking northward to escape Shaka's demonic rule. These refugees themselves were hardly gentle, and as they moved away from Zululand they left a trail of devastation behind. By 1830, the Nguni people, related to the Zulu but driven out by them, entered the southern frontiers of the Rozwi land. Though they once had been the finest warriors of the continent, the long-settled Rozwi were no match for these barbaric nomads. The Nguni swarmed through the cities of the Rozwi like a ravening horde of locusts devouring a harvest.

Zimbabwe was one of the first places to be attacked. The

Nguni had no interest in golden trinkets; they simply sacked the city, slaughtered its inhabitants, burned everything, and moved on. Chirisamuru, the last of the Rozwi Mambos, was holding court at Manyanga, "the place of the tusks," a hundred miles northwest of Zimbabwe. Nguni marauders led by the ferocious Zwangendaba Kumalo came to Manyanga in 1834. The proud Mambo, heir to a royal line more than four centuries old, awaited Zwangendaba's coming calmly and was flayed alive in his palace. The following year, the Nguni completed their destruction of the Rozwi and passed north of the Zambezi River en route to new depredations.

The shattered Rozwi crept back to ruined Zimbabwe. They could not occupy the pillaged buildings, because they were now infested by the *ngozi,* the dangerous spirits of murdered tribesmen who had not received proper burial. Instead, the returning Rozwi cobbled together a few new dwellings, flimsy and crude, and tried to carry on their ancient ceremonies. It proved to be impossible. The priests were dead; the rites had been forgotten. One by one the Rozwi drifted away to settle among other tribes. In the end, only a few old men remained at Zimbabwe, such as Babareke, who introduced himself to Mauch and wistfully begged the German to bring him knowledge of how to offer the right sort of sacrifices to the high god.

Then came the treasure hunters—and after them the archeologists, who solved the mystery of Zimbabwe, not without some detours and false turns.

There is no "myth" of Zimbabwe today. The work of David Randall-MacIver, Gertrude Caton-Thompson, Roger Summers, and others in this century has laid to rest the old legend that Zimbabwe was King Solomon's Ophir. Phoenician seamen may well have visited the coasts of Africa thirty centuries ago, but they did not build the stone towers of Zimbabwe. Only a few die-hard and unlettered white Rhodesians cling to the belief that men of their own race *must* have been the builders. To them, living as an uneasy minority ruling a black multitude crying out for independence, the Phoenician origin of Zimbabwe is practically a matter of religious faith. But those who are less emotionally involved in the Rhodesian situation are willing to accept the carbon-14 findings and the historical data filtered from the tribal legends.

The sequence of events that unrolled during Zimbabwe's twenty centuries is by no means completely clear today, as Roger Summers would be the first to admit. Africa's climate is not as kind to acheologists as that of the Near East, and many vital links in the chain of evidence have rotted away, while others were destroyed by the clumsy excavators of the late nineteenth century. But the general pattern of the Zimbabwe story is secure.

First came the Bushmen, unknown thousands of years ago, and then the Iron Age miners who worked the rich gold deposits. They left, eventually to be replaced by the Shona-speaking founders of the Monomotapa state. At the time when Portuguese navigators first were venturing down the African coast, another powerful African realm, that of the Rozwi, rose to challenge the Monomotapa and ultimately triumphed and took possession of Great Zimbabwe.

The Rozwi held it and embellished it for hundreds of years. Then came the torches of the Nguni, and by 1834 Zimbabwe was in ruins. And afterward arrived white men who talked of Phoenicians and Sabaeans.

To archeologists today, the noisy controversy over Zimbabwe's origin is a thing of the past, a closed chapter. Gallons of ink were spilled at the turn of this century to prove that Zimbabwe was thousands of years old, and arguments were put forth that seem incredible now in the light of the evidence at hand. The tourists who come to Zimbabwe these days stare in awe at the splendid stone walls and towers, as well they might, and let themselves succumb to the temptation to believe that all this is enormously ancient, a relic of the dawn of time. Yet—ironically—the finishing touches had been put to Zimbabwe's walls less than a century before Mauch and Hall and the rest began insisting that the city of stone was the Biblical Ophir, already old in King Solomon's day.

Five

Mexico: Aztecs And Others

WHEN the bearded white strangers landed on the eastern coast, King Moctezuma of the Aztecs felt no surprise. There had been omens. In A.D. 1510 the waters of Lake Texcoco boiled and rose in quiet weather and poured into the streets of the capital. The following year a temple burst into flames without cause, and the blaze could not be extinguished. Three comets flashed through the skies, one of them in daylight. A column of fire appeared by night in the east. The sleep of the terrified Aztecs was broken by the sound of a woman wailing in the streets of Tenochtitlán, the mother-goddess sobbing for her children. Animals in labor produced monsters. Two-headed men were seen in the provinces. Fishermen captured an ash-gray crane with a mirror set in its forehead and brought it to Moctezuma. He stared into the mirror by day and saw the gleaming stars of the sky. He looked again and saw men in the costume of war, carried on the backs of deer. The royal soothsayers could offer no explanations. But Moctezuma knew that strange omens foretold even stranger events to come in Mexico.

The Aztec monarch lived under the shadow of a prophecy. Long ago there had been a king named Quetzalcoatl in the city of Tollán. He had been a man of peace, beloved by all, but enemies arose and drove him into exile. With his followers he made his way to the shore of the Gulf of Mexico and put out to sea on a raft of serpents, journeying to some unknown eastern land. The prophecy said that one day Quetzalcoatl would return: a fair-skinned man, with long hair and a black beard. No longer a man but now a god, Quetzalcoatl would assume royal power once more in Mexico.

[109]

In 1518 came a messenger from the coast. "A great mountain has been seen upon the waters, moving from one part to the other, without touching the rocks," he told Moctezuma. The king sent two trusted men to verify the story. They returned and said it was true, that men with white skins and thick black beards had arrived in "a house on the water" and had come ashore.

Quetzalcoatl had returned, Moctezuma knew. He ordered food and rich gifts to be offered to the god-king and his retinue, and it was done. But Quetzalcoatl did not stay. The bearded ones returned to their vessel and departed, leaving behind some biscuits on the beach. Moctezuma had them reverently gathered up, wrapped in embroidered cloths, and carried to the sacred city of Tollán by chanting priests, who buried the holy relics at Quetzalcoatl's ruined temple. Soon, Moctezuma knew, Quetzalcoatl would land on the Mexican shore again, and this time he would come to stay. The Aztec king prepared to yield up the great power that was his, when that time came.

But the bearded visitors of 1518 were not gods. They were Spaniards under the command of Juan de Grijalva, on a voyage of reconnaissance out of Cuba. They did not yet know of the wealth of this land of Mexico, although the gifts of Moctezuma startled and delighted them: jewelry, precious stones, capes of feathers; above all, gold. They were the forerunners of the armada of conquest under Hernando Cortés that arrived the following year. Unable to comprehend the words of the Aztec messengers, Grijalva's men did not realize that Moctezuma had already virtually handed his wealthy land over to them.

He had instructed his emissaries to tell Quetzalcoatl to allow him to die in peace: "After my death he will be welcome to come here and take possession of his kingdom, as it is his. We know that he left it to be guarded by my ancestors, and I have always considered that my domain was only lent to me. Let him permit me to end my days here. Then let him return to enjoy what is his!"

Since they could not understand those words, the Spaniards did not then know that Moctezuma was welcoming them as returning gods. But soon enough Mexico would be theirs, first of the three great Indian civilizations of Middle America to topple before Spanish greed.

In the jutting thumb of a peninsula that is Yucatán lived the Mayas, whose civilization had existed unbroken for some fifteen hundred years. They did not form an empire, only a loose confederation of city-states, and by 1546 the Spaniards ruled them. Far to the south, in Peru, was the gigantic realm of the Incas, assembled by conquest late in the fifteenth century and a victim of Spanish treachery within sixty years after reaching its peak. The Incas fell to bloody Pizarro in 1533. But the Aztecs, the most warlike Indians of all, went first. By 1521, their spectacularly rapid rise had brought them to an even more spectacularly rapid catastrophe at the hands of the men they thought were gods.

The Aztecs were the last in a remarkable series of Indian civilizations in Mexico. Because they and the Incas had attained such greatness by the time the Spanish arrived, we often assume that both these imperial states were ancient. Actually, both were upstarts whose lineage went back at best a few centuries. The task of archeologists in Mexico has been not to reconstruct the Aztec civilization, which was richly documented by the conquering Spaniards themselves, but to search for the roots of Mexican culture in the distant past.

That pre-Aztec Mexican past has been of vital concern to students of man's development in the Americas. Within Mexico's borders certain tribes first crossed the threshold from food gatherers to food producers and set in motion the wave of progress that culminated in Moctezuma's glorious city of Tenochtitlán, in Chichén Itzá of the Mayas, in the opulent Inca capital of Cuzco, in all the grandeur and complexity that went down under Spanish steel four centuries ago.

The ancestors of the Aztecs and all other American Indians came out of Asia, crossing the fifty-six-mile Bering Strait about twenty or thirty thousand years ago. These migrants moved in small family groups and arrived a few at a time over a long period. They spread slowly out over both the Americas, reaching as far south as Cape Horn.

They were nomads at first. They hunted the big animals, the mastodons, bison, and camels that still roamed the land, and they varied their diet with roots and seeds. They built no villages and raised no crops. But about eight thousand years ago, perhaps a little earlier, the climate began to change. It grew dry, and thickly forested country became desert. The large mammals died out. The hunting life became more difficult. The nomads adapted, and some settled down. In Mexico, they invented agriculture.

Mexico was the funnel through which the Indians had reached South America, and some remained. The high, dry Mexican plateau was attractive to nomadic hunters. Mexico offers all ranges of climate, from torrid jungles on the coasts to icy wastes at the summits of the high volcanos, but much of the country is a huge inland plateau set off by two mountain chains.

The American Indians had an extensive repertoire of crops by the time of the European discoveries, and nearly everything they raised was unique to the New World. Only cotton, yams, certain gourds, and the coconut were products common to both hemispheres. Only in the Americas were such things cultivated as white and sweet potatoes, chili peppers, lima beans, pumpkins, peanuts, tomatoes, avocados, tobacco, and pineapples. But the basic foodstuff was corn. The Old World had wheat, millet, rye, oats, and barley, all descended from wild grasses. In the New World, corn took the place of those crops.

Corn was the foundation of the great Indian cultures. Hundreds of different types, adapted to growing conditions of all sorts from tropic to arctic, were raised in the two continents. The bounty of corn freed many people for tasks other than food gathering, since a relative handful of farmers could produce enough corn to feed many people. That left hands and minds unencumbered to invent new ways of doing things. The wonderful arithmetic of the corn yield led the way to a breathtakingly rapid expansion of Indian culture in the most favored regions.

But where did it start? Indian corn, *Zea mays,* is not a wild plant. Its seeds, its kernels, are sheltered behind tough husks, and without the help of man those seeds cannot reach the soil. Obviously, ancient farmers had practiced a kind of artificial selection that created a highly edible kernel and a species unable to disperse its seeds unaided. One of the long-standing puzzles of Mexican archeology was to find the ancestral wild grass that had been turned into Indian corn.

Two candidates suggested themselves, both grassy weeds that

showed definite kinship to modern corn. These were teosinte and *Tripsacum,* both found in a natural state in the Mexican and Central American highlands. During the 1940's, studies by Paul C. Mangelsdorf of Harvard University and other researchers showed that neither of these could be the ancestor of corn. *Tripsacum* was a cousin of corn, not an ancestor; and teosinte was a fairly recent accidential hybrid between domestic corn and *Tripsacum.* Mangelsdorf suggested that the true ancestor of corn would turn out to be a kind of popcorn, with its kernels encased in pods.

Archeologists set about the search. In 1953, cores of earth brought up by drilling into the old lake beds on which Mexico City stands produced grains of corn pollen 80,000 years old. This was the ancestral wild corn that had grown in Mexico thousands of years before the first human settlers reached the New World. The quest now turned to the desert area stretching from the American Southwest to southern Mexico. In 1948, small corncobs of great age were found in Bat Cave, New Mexico. Carbon-14 dating showed them to be almost 6,000 years old. Not long afterward, corncobs almost equally ancient were discovered in a cave in the arid state of Tamaulipas, in northeast Mexico.

The finder of the Tamaulipas corncobs was Richard S. Mac-Neish, a one-time amateur boxing champion who had taken degrees in anthropology, archeology, and ethnology at the University of Chicago. In 1949 MacNeish became chief archeologist for the National Museum of Canada, under whose auspices he continued his search for the ancestor of corn. Tamaulipas, which is practically without rain, seemed like a good place to look. The dry climate would preserve any ancient corncobs or kernels. But several years of work failed to add any new light. MacNeish came upon a good deal of early corn, generally about 4,500 years old, but it was similar to modern popcorn. The strata below the corn-bearing layers held the relics of a food-gathering people who had occupied the region from about 5000 B.C. They used stone tools and weapons, hunted deer, jaguar, and wild pigs for meat, and obtained the bulk of their food by collecting nuts, seeds, plant stems, and even insects. At this early date they had already begun to cultivate corn in a small way, raising a tiny-eared variety that they chewed raw, roasted, popped, and ground into meal.

The explorations in Tamaulipas produced some surprises—notably one site that yielded carbon-14 dates of 6544 B.C. ± 450 years, and where some cultivation of pumpkins and peppers seemed to have taken place. This was one of the earliest known farming sites of the New World. Indeed, it showed that agriculture was nearly as ancient in the Americas as in the Old World, since only a few extraordinary Old World sites such as Jericho had produced evidence of earlier cultivation.

MacNeish still was after the ancestor of corn, since that was the dominant Indian crop. Not having found it north of Mexico City, he moved his base of operations to an equally dry zone in Mexico's southern highlands. By trial and error he narrowed the possibilities to three desert areas in the states of Oaxaca, Guerrero, and Puebla.

When he discovered nothing revealing in Oaxaca, he tried the Valley of Tehuacán in southeastern Puebla. The first thirty-eight caves were unfruitful, but in the thirty-ninth, Coxcatlán, MacNeish found three unusually primitive-looking corncobs in February, 1960. Carbon-14 analysis at the University of Michigan showed that they were five hundred years older than any corn yet found in the New World. Now a large-scale expedition was launched; more than fifty scientists eventually became involved, specialists in fields as varied as geography, zoology, genetics, geology, and botany.

They detected twenty-eight separate levels of occupation in the cave, the oldest dating from about 10,000 B.C. Except for the years from 2300 to 900 B.C., Coxcatlán had been inhabited continuously from the earliest settlement of Mexico until the coming of the Spaniards—a span of almost twelve thousand years. Eleven other caves in the valley also produced valuable finds. "In four seasons of digging from 1961 to 1964," MacNeish wrote,

we reaped a vast archaeological harvest. This includes nearly a million individual remains of human activity, more than 1,000 animal bones (including those of extinct antelopes and horses), 80,000 individual wild-plant remains and some 25,000 specimens of corn. The artifacts arrange themselves into significant sequences of stone tools, textiles and pottery. They provide an almost continuous picture of the rise of civilization in the valley of Tehuacán.

The expedition's specialists were able to sketch the changes in environment, climate, and plant and animal life during the twelve thousand years, working from the geological evidence, from pollen traces in the caves, from such things as the shells of land snails, and from other relics. It was even possible to determine the seasons of the year at which many of the cave floors had been occupied, by analyzing the types of plant remains found in them.

MacNeish had struck archeological gold in a Coxcatlán cave: tiny corncobs, "no bigger than the filter tip of a cigarette . . . , but under a magnifying lens one could see that they were indeed miniature ears of corn, with sockets that had once contained kernels enclosed in pods. These cobs proved to be some 7,000 years old. Mangelsdorf is convinced that this must be wild corn—the original parent from which modern corn is descended."

Through such painstaking work, carried out under cruel desert conditions in remote caves, the beginnings of Mexican civilization have been charted. First came the early hunters and food gatherers, who scratched out a meager existence in the Mexican highlands from about 12,000 B.C. to about 7000 B.C. Then began what is known as the Archaic Period, in which these people shifted from hunting and trapping to being mainly collectors of plant foods. They learned how to raise squash and a few other plants themselves, and during the growing season they remained fixed in one place, tending their crops. Most of their food, though, still came haphazardly as they found it in the wilds.

About 5000 B.C. some ten per cent of the food supply was derived from domesticated plants: beans, peppers, squash, and the newly domesticated corn. As their farming skills increased, they found ways of breeding better kinds of corn with bigger ears. These hybrids could not disperse their own seeds, so the farmers had to collect and plant them, then cultivate the fields with digging sticks, pull weeds, supply water when necessary. Now each tribal group had its own planting ground, and it stayed put. The old nomadic ways disappeared. The people built the first permanent villages, living in small pits in the ground covered with wooden roofs. By about 3400 B.C., a third of the food supply came from agriculture, and the yield was so high that the pace of development speeded up.

The idea of agriculture—and particularly the techniques of breeding and raising corn—spread to other parts of Mexico, to South America, and to the American Southwest. Mexico had a head start of several thousand years, though, and it was there that the first really complex cultures evolved.

Archeologists call this culture-building period in Mexico the Formative Period and date its beginning at about 1500 B.C. The Formative is defined as the epoch of effective village life based on the cultivation of corn, beans, and squash, and marked by the use of pottery, the loom, carefully ground stone tools, and a developed religious and artistic capacity indicated by the fashioning of clay figurines. This was a period of great population expansion, thanks to the bounty of corn, and with the doubling and redoubling of the population came a rush of new ideas and techniques.

Most of what is known of the Formative has been uncovered in the area of greatest Mexican archeological activity: the Valley of Mexico. This is where the most powerful Mexican civilizations flourished in later centuries. The Valley of Mexico is a natural basin covering some three thousand square miles, at an altitude of a mile and a half, bounded by ranges of towering volcanic mountains. Once this region was largely covered by a vast shallow lake, which had already begun to disappear in Aztec times and today is represented only by a few isolated ponds. In Formative times, actually, the Valley of Mexico was something of a backward region, and the real vanguard of progress was in the southern and central highlands. But because several great cultures of later times lived in the Valley, most of the excavations have taken place there.

The Formative villages there were established near the shores of the great lake. A typical Middle Formative village was uncovered in 1936 at Tlatilco while a brickworks was excavating in clay deposits. About 800 B.C., Tlatilco covered about 160 acres. Its people were fishermen and hunters as well as farmers, and the Tlatilco women were superb potters who produced excellent figurines and pots. There is an oddly grotesque flavor to much of this Tlatilco work: the figurines depict monstrosities with two heads, or with extra eyes and noses, or with horrifying ugly faces. Many of the figures are deformed. Some eerie masks are split lengthwise into two different faces, one bare to the bone, the other idiotic, with bulging eyes and outthrust tongue. These unusual clay objects bear a marked resemblance to the sort of pottery being produced at just about that time by the Chavín culture of Peru. So many points of similarity exist between the Chavín and Tlatilco peoples that archeologists regard it as certain that there was contact between Mexico and Peru about 800 B.C. Probably the travelers went by ocean-going rafts or canoes, since no artifacts of this type have been discovered along any of the possible overland routes between the two culture centers.

Another key site of early Mexican civilization is Monte Albán, in the earthquake-harried Mexican state of Oaxaca, south of Veracruz. Three great valleys meet at the city of Oaxaca, and a short automobile ride from the city brings one to Monte Albán, constructed on high ground about a thousand feet above the valley of the Atoyac River.

This is the territory of the Zapotec and Mixtec Indians, two groups who managed to avoid the Aztec sledge hammer and to survive the Spaniards as well. They have occupied this part of Mexico for centuries. Most of the buildings at Monte Albán are Zapotec work; some are those of the Mixtecs, who infiltrated the region about A.D. 1350.

The oldest Monte Albán ruins, at the southwest corner of the site, go back to the Formative Period. These pre-Zapotec deposits show the influence of the Olmecs (still another culture) to some degree, but they evidently are the work of a separate though possibly related group.

A second phase at Monte Albán lasted from perhaps 200 B.C. to A.D. 300 and marked the transition from the Formative Period to what archeologists term Mexico's Classic Period. An arrowhead-shaped building made up of dark, narrow chambers is the best Monte Albán II site. It, too, contains inscriptions, whose symbols show mountains, towns, and upside-down heads decked with showy headdresses. Alfonso Caso of the National Museum of Mexico, the chief archeologist of Monte Albán, has suggested that these are the records of conquered towns, each inverted head standing for a defeated king.

The Classic Period, which lasted from A.D. 300 to A.D. 900, was Mexico's golden age. It was a time of relative peace, when the arts of civilization could flourish. Where there had been towns, now there were great cities as mighty as any of Europe. Imposing temples and pyramids were constructed in many parts of the country. Systems of writing were devised. Pottery attained a level of perfection matched only in Peru, among all New World cultures. Though they made no use of wheeled vehicles, the civilizations of Mexico at this time were otherwise as complex and sophisticated as any in the world.

At Monte Albán, the new era, Phase III, was the work of the Zapotecs. They built all up and down the Valley of Oaxaca, constructing hundreds of temples, tombs, and ball courts where a game something like basketball was played. The underground tombs of the Zapotec aristocracy were vaulted chambers adorned with handsome frescoes showing processions of the gods. The elite of Monte Albán inhabited the heights, while the peasants dwelled in the valley; class distinctions were sharp in the Mexico of Classic times.

At Cholula, in what is now the state of Puebla, work began on the largest man-made structure of the pre-Columbian New World: a colossal pyramid, rising to a height of about 180 feet and covering 25 acres at the base. Today the Cholula Pyramid seems to be no more than a large hill, topped by a Spanish church. But the entire mound was built by hand, from sun-dried mud bricks about fifteen inches long, set in a mortar of clay. Its base, 1,440 feet on a side, was twice the length of the base of the Great Pyramid of Khufu in Egypt. When the Spaniards first came to Cholula in 1519, Bernal Díaz, a scholarly conquistador, counted 120 steps leading up the side of the Cholula Pyramid to the temple at its top. The Spaniards wrote a dark page of their history at Cholula, launching a surprise attack on the natives and setting fire to the temple on the pyramid when they took refuge there. When a Spanish traveler visited Cholula in 1744, he found the pyramid "so covered with earth and shrubs that it seems rather a natural hill than an edifice," and no trace of the steps remained.

[118]

Partial archeological examination has revealed that the structure was built in four stages, all during the Classic Period, and reached its final bulk about A.D. 900 or 1000.

The dominant city of Mexico's Classic Period was Teotihuacán, in a valley northeast of the Valley of Mexico proper. It was a ceremonial center rather than a true city. Its site covers three square miles and could have supported some 25,000 people in the heyday of Teotihuacán, but everything about the ruins shows that it was a place of worship to which the faithful came to celebrate the festivals of planting and harvest and the rites of the gods. Long after Teotihuacán was an abandoned ghost city, Mexicans made pilgrimages to it; doomed Moctezuma himself came there on foot several times. From Teotihuacán ruled the overlords of the first great civilization of the Valley of Mexico.

The city was laid out on a grid, with the streets oriented 15 to 17 degrees east of true north—evidently of mystic significance, since the arrangement was followed elsewhere in the Valley. Its main road, the Avenue of the Dead, stretched almost two miles from the Pyramid of the Moon to the Temple of Quetzalcoatl, a grand processionway bounded by public buildings of great majesty. Rising above all else, just to the east of the Avenue of the Dead, was the tremendous Pyramid of the Sun, more than two hundred feet high, its sides seven hundred feet long at the base. Bricks of mud, a million cubic yards of them, went into the making of this pyramid. Once it was faced with stone, and an awesome stone stairway led to the thatch-roofed wooden temple at the summit.

Palaces and temples abounded, everything decorated with colored frescoes and intricate carvings. All the gods of Mexico had their shrines here, the Feathered Serpent, Quetzalcoatl, and the gods of the sun, the moon, the rain, the harvest. At the eastern part of the site, away from all the splendor, archeologists found a pell-mell cluster of rooms and narrow alleys, most likely the dwellings of the humble artisans and sweepers and masons who kept the city in good repair.

It was a city of unparalleled grandeur. In its sun-washed courts and atop its looming pyramids were performed rites of barbaric cruelty, for the gods loved the taste of blood, and all this magnificence was designed to give lives to the hungry deities. The blinding radiance of Teotihuacán dazzled all Mexico for three hundred years, and the gods were well served. We do not know who the builders of the city were. They were not the Zapotecs of Monte Albán. They may have been the Totonacs from Veracruz, or they may have been the forerunners of the Nahua-speaking groups who gave rise to the Aztecs. There is no clue.

About A.D. 600, unknown enemies came to Teotihuacán and destroyed it—a dark episode that slashes across the brightness of Classic Mexico. The opulent palaces were wrecked and burned, and the elegant pottery and sculpture of Teotihuacán no longer went forth to other districts. Primitive squatters lived in the ruins for three centuries more, flinging their own flimsy huts above the shattered splendor.

Then a convulsion shook all of Mexico, and the death that had come to Teotihuacán finally found the rest of the Classic states about the year 900. Some terrible pattern of events sent a shiver through the entire land, reaching even the Mayas, in remote Guatemala and Honduras, and driving them to abandon their monumental stone cities, drawing back fearfully into their heartland of Yucatán.

There may have been a drought so severe it shriveled the souls of men. Perhaps revolution swept the cities as the downtrodden ones at last rebelled at rearing palaces and temples for their masters. Certainly barbarians came knocking at the gateway to Mexico. It was a time of fear, of change and upheaval. Fortresses rose for the first time, and brawling armies collided in the hills. The gods were well fed, for the blood of prisoners streamed in rivers. New states emerged. The Zapotecs fled from Monte Albán; Cholula labored under the lash of conquerers.

From the north, from desert country so savage that agriculture had never been born there, nomads called the Chichimecs, the "dog people," fell upon Mexico. Some of these Chichimec tribes knew only how to destroy, but one wave of migration brought with it a new cultural stock that rose to supremacy as the Teotihuacán people had done earlier.

These were the Toltecs, a tribe of quick learners. Aztec tradition says that they came from the far west and moved by stages into civilized Mexico, pausing for several years at a time and picking up such practices of civilization as were useful to them. By A.D. 980, a Toltec leader named Mixcoatl, "Cloud Serpent," brought them into central Mexico. Mixcoatl's son and successor was Topiltzín, born about A.D. 935. He was destined to be more than a king; he became the god Quetzalcoatl.

The worship of Quetzalcoatl goes back before the Toltec arrival, and its origins are lost in the haze of years. A feathered serpent was his emblem; he was the god who had brought art and culture to mankind, the true teacher, the founder of civilization. Alone among the gods of Mexico, Quetzalcoatl drank no blood. He abhorred human sacrifice and was honored only with offerings of snakes and butterflies. He was the high god of Teotihuacán and the shining symbol of the radiant Classic Period of Mexico.

Now, in the strife-torn era of the Post-Classic Period ushered in by the fall of the old civilizations, Topiltzín of the Toltecs somehow became identified with Quetzalcoatl. He advocated peace and lived a saintly life in a harsh era. His wicked uncle murdered King Mixcoatl and usurped the Toltec throne; when Topiltzín-Quetzalcoatl reached manhood, he slew the false monarch on the Hill of the Star and took his rightful place at the head of his nation.

The young king drew craftsmen from Puebla and the Gulf Coast, men who knew the old ways, and they built him a new capital, Tollán or Tula. Just where this city actually was is open to question. Many places in Mexico have that name today, for it seems to have meant no more than "the city." Recent archeological work has shown that the Tula of Topiltzín was northwest of the Valley of Mexico, in the state of Hidalgo.

That Tula was quite thoroughly ruined. Its pyramids and ball courts and colonnaded halls show the careful work of dedicated vandals. Its palaces are no more than stumps, but their floor plans indicate that they were patterned after great Teotihuacán. The altars show the Feathered Serpent everywhere. But a sinister note, alien to Quetzalcoatl's philosophy, is struck by the decorations of the city's final phase; skulls and crossbones ornament the altars, and there are carved representations of the sacred vessels designed to receive throbbing human hearts after the sacrifice.

The evidence supports the myths. Aztec legends declare that the saintly King Topiltzín had fierce enemies, the devotees of the bloodthirsty death-god Tezcatlipoca. Civil war raged in Tula between the forces of life and the forces of death, and Topiltzín and his supporters were driven into exile, leaving the city to the partisans of human sacrifice. Weeping, the banished king walked through the valleys and over the snowy mountain passes, birds of bright plumage showing the way, until he came to the Gulf of Mexico. Then, one story says, he lit a funeral pyre for himself and strode into it, wearing his cloak of feathers and his mask of turquoise, and his heart became the morning star, his ashes turned to green-feathered quetzal birds. But the most common version, well known to the Aztecs, told of his departure for unknown lands in the east aboard a raft of twined serpents. "I am called hence," Topiltzín-Quetzalcoatl told his followers. "The sun hath called me." But he vowed to return one day, this fair-skinned, black-bearded king who was a god.

Topiltzín's fall is traditionally set in A.D. 987. It is confirmed by Mayan traditions that tell of the arrival in Yucatán that year of the god Kukulcan, white of skin and dark of beard, who claimed to be an exile from Tula in the north. They threw him in the Sacred Well of Chichén Itzá as a sacrifice, but he did not drown, so they hauled him out and made him their ruler. Images of feathered serpents came to decorate the Mayan cities. Then, here too, the living god disappeared, vowing to return one day. The treacherous legend helped to smooth the way for the Spanish conquest of the Mayas, just as it did in Aztec Mexico.

What we have here, it would seem, is an accurate historical episode transfigured by myth. There must have been a civil war among the Toltecs, and the faction of peace was cast out. The exiles went to Yucatán, leaving unmistakable traces of their presence in the Mayan cities. The remaining Toltecs continued to expand their empire until most of Mexico paid tribute to Tula.

The curtain dropped for the Toltecs in the middle of the twelfth century. Drought and internal feuding weakened them, and Tula fell to invaders. Huémac, the last Toltec ruler, moved his capital to the hill of Chapultepec in what now is the western part of Mexico City, and there he took his own life. In 1168—the year is traditional—the Toltecs were dispersed, some straggling to places like Cholula, others taking refuge among the Mayas where Quetzalcoatl had gone in an earlier century.

New disturbances racked Mexico now. More of the barbaric Chichimec tribes flooded in from the north. Of all the earlier peoples, the only ones still maintaining a semblance of their former life were the Zapotecs of Oaxaca. Though they had abandoned their capital at Monte Albán, the Zapotecs had built a new city twenty-five miles away at Mitla, where Zapotec rites are celebrated to this day. But they were under pressure from the Mixtecs, a tribe out of the desert highlands of western Oaxaca.

The collapse of the Toltecs in 1168 had left the northern half of the Valley of Mexico at the mercy of the Chichimecs. As had happened nearly three hundred years before, they came in waves, sacking and destroying all they encountered before settling down to learn more refined behavior from the remnants of the peoples they invaded. Eventually the newcomers founded cities of their own or took over existing ones. The Acolhuas founded the city of Texcoco, on the east side of the great lake of that name. On the western shore of Lake Texcoco was the city of Azcapotzalco, occupied by the descendants of refugees from fallen Teotihuacán. A powerful tribe called the Tepanecs seized Azcapotzalco and expanded it greatly. South of Lake Texcoco, survivors of the Toltec disaster built a town called Colhuacán and attempted to retain their old level of culture in the face of this barbarian tide. Several other city-states also emerged around Lake Texcoco and its environs. During the thirteenth century these small, newly founded states, Chichimec in the north and Toltec in the south, tested one another's strength and entered into rapidly shifting alliances. The power of the northern states grew; the Tepanec city of Azcapotzalco became the mightiest force west of the lake, while its rival on the other shore, the Acolhua city of Texcoco, drew tribute from seventy towns.

About 1300, poverty-stricken wanderers from someplace in the northwest of Mexico began to enter the Valley. They were land-less, backward, having few skills except those of war. They were known as the Mexicas, but they also called themselves the Aztecs, from the name of their legendary place or origin, Aztlan.

The current residents of the Valley of Mexico, themselves only two or three generations up from barbarism, looked with disdain and resentment at this shabby tribe of nomads. There is no snob-bery like that of a newly civilized culture, and the Tepanecs and Acolhuas and others despised the Aztecs because they saw them-selves of a hundred years before mirrored in the ragged invaders. They mocked the Aztecs and drove them away wherever they tried to settle.

The Aztecs wandered on through the Valley of Mexico, fol-lowing the priests who carried the image of their tribal god, Huitzilopochtli, "Divine Lord of War." He was a god who re-quired much blood, and the Aztecs were bound by claims of piety to present him regularly with the hearts of captive warriors, which did not endear them to the citizens of the Valley. At last the Aztecs came as far south as Colhuacán, whose people, Toltec refugees, could claim three hundred years of civilization. They had no psychological need to spurn the Aztecs and took them on as serfs and as a kind of mercenary army to protect them. The Aztecs settled on the outskirts of Colhuacán and lived on scraps from the tables of Colhuacán for a while.

In 1323, the king of Colhuacán made a friendly gesture as a bond between the two groups: he sent his Aztec serfs a royal princess as a bride for their leader. The Aztecs, flattered, paid the young lady the highest compliment they knew: they sacri-ficed her to Huitzilopochtli, hoping that the god would accept her as a tribal goddess. Obsidian knives flashed, a throbbing heart was ripped from a living body, and the Colhuacán princess was flayed so that her skin could be worn by a priest at the festivals of the new goddess.

The people of Colhuacán failed to appreciate the honor paid to the princess. They rose in anger against the loathsome Aztec savages and drove them out. For two years the Aztecs wandered once again through the swampy reed-covered islands along the western shore of Lake Texcoco. Their priests told them to roam until they came to a cactus sprouting from a rock, on which an eagle would be perched with a snake grasped in his beak. The requirement was fulfilled, according to Aztec legend, and at the place where they spied the four omens in conjunction they built their town. They called it Tenochtitlán, Place of the Cactus in the Rock.

It was no more than a muddy shantytown on a dismal cluster of islands. But the Aztecs had lived at Colhuacán long enough to absorb some valuable ideas, and they proceeded to employ them now with brilliant effect. What they had learned was the system of agriculture and swamp drainage known as *chinampa*, which had been practiced on the shores of the Valley of Mexico's vast lake at least since the beginning of the Classic Period in A.D. 300.

Tourists who visit Mexico today invariably pay a visit to the most famous remaining center of chinampa agriculture, at the town of Xochimilco south of Mexico City. Here are the "floating gardens," which do not float at all, though guides will insist that once they did. The legend of the floating gardens seems to have been fathered by José Acosta, whose *Natural and Moral History of the Indies* was published in 1590. He wrote:

Those who have not seen the seed gardens that are constructed on the lake of Mexico, in the midst of the waters, will take what is described here as a fabulous story, or at best will believe it to be an enchantment of the devil, to whom these people paid worship. But in reality the matter is entirely feasible. Gardens that move on the water have been built by piling earth on sedges and reeds in such a manner that the water does not destroy them, and on these gardens they plant and cultivate, and plants grow and ripen, and they tow these gardens from one place to another.

Actually chinampas are and always have been long, narrow strips of land bordered by canals and thoroughly rooted to the earth below. The farmers cut masses of water vegetation loose and tow them as living rafts to the chinampas, dumping them for compost, and this is what must have led Acosta astray. The chinampas of Xochimilco, which survive today chiefly as a tourist attraction, were built long before the Aztecs appeared. Each one is about three hundred feet long and fifteen to thirty feet wide, and they are laid out on a large grid tilted 15 to 17 degrees east of true north—the same arrangement as the streets of Teotihuacán, indicating possible astrological significance.

Before the chinampas, Xochimilco was swampland. The builders created this gridwork of canals, draining the land, and the mud dug out in cutting the canals was piled between them to lift the surface of the chinampas above the water level. Trees were planted to anchor the soil. Then, each year, fresh mud was dug from the canal bottom and spread on the garden plot, and water weeds were added as fertilizer.

The Aztecs built chinampas with a will when they arrived in 1325, drained their swamps, and constructed causeways to connect the separate islands. Tenochtitlán grew explosively. The former beggars suddenly were masters of a powerful island state and attracted the attention of the same Tepanecs who had spurned them earlier. The Tepanecs of Azcapotzalco, determined to assert their power over the other city-states of the Valley, saw in the Aztecs a useful ally.

Tezozomoc, the ruler of Azcapotzalco, accepted the Aztecs as satellites and gave his daughter in marriage to the Aztec king, who did not repeat the mistake that had been made with the princess from Colhuacán. Together, the Tepanecs and their Aztec vassals conquered nearly all their neighbors. The only state that remained independent was wealthy Texcoco, across the lake from Azcapotzalco. Tezozomoc had saved his great rival for the last.

The Tepanec king was past ninety when he finally launched his offensive against Texcoco in 1416. Tepanecs of Azcapotzalco and Aztecs of Tenochtitlán fought side by side, laying siege to Texcoco, invading it, slaughtering its citizens. Texcoco's king was slain, but a royal prince, Nezahualcóyotl, escaped into the mountains. The incredibly aged Tezozomoc hunted him like Ahab stalking the White Whale, but Nezahualcóyotl remained at large, a symbol of Texcoco's survival.

At the age of 106, Tezozomoc of Azcapotzalco died, in 1426. Instantly came a shift in the political structure of the Valley of Mexico. The seemingly endless reign of the old man had bred discontent among the impatient heirs, a pack of frustrated middle-aged princes. One of them, Maxtlatzin, hungered for the throne more than most and murdered his brother, who had succeeded Tezozomoc. It was not a popular move in Azcapotzalco. The usurper particularly feared that his Aztec vassals might object and rebel against him. So he arranged for the assassination of the Aztec king as the first step in reducing the power of these suddenly formidable neighbors.

The scheme backfired. The Aztecs rose in revolt, and their new king allied himself with the exiled Nezahualcóyotl of Texcoco. The people of Texcoco, demoralized since their defeat eleven years before, sprang to new vigor as their legendary prince returned. Fleets of canoes crossed Lake Texcoco and Azcapotzalco was invaded by a joint army from Texcoco and Tenochtitlán. Maxtlatzin was taken, the Tepanecs were utterly crushed, and Azcapotzalco was left in ruins. By thoughtful maneuvering the Aztecs had made themselves one of the two great powers of the Valley of Mexico in less than a century, starting from nothing.

Nezahualcóyotl returned in glory to Texcoco, took a hundred wives, and reigned magnificently for many years. Across the lake, Tenochtitlán flourished. More swampland was reclaimed, whole new blocks of buildings appeared, and the palaces of the high Aztec leaders grew ever more splendid. By the late fifteenth century, the population of Tenochtitlán was greater than a quarter of a million. London had 120,000 people then. In Spain, Christopher Columbus was attempting to raise funds for an expedition by sea to Asia, and that would have some effect on Tenochtitlán's future growth, but the Aztecs knew nothing of Columbus, or of Spain, or of what the future might hold, other than ever-increasing grandeur.

The Aztec economy had long been based on the fertility of the chinampas. Even now, though dozens of cities paid tribute in food to the Aztecs, they still needed to maintain their own productivity, and that involved them in some complicated engineering projects. Landlocked Lake Texcoco and its adjoining lakes were shrinking through evaporation, and as the water level receded the concentration of deadly salts assumed greater proportions. Fresh-water springs feeding into the lakes kept the water pure. Now, with the chinampas multiplying at a time when dry weather was causing the level of the water to drop, the

Aztecs began to build huge aqueducts to carry fresh water from mainland sources to the lake. The first of these great covered conduits of stone was completed in the generation after the fall of Azcapotzalco, during the reign of the important Aztec king Moctezuma I (1440–1468). It carried the flow from a spring at the foot of Chapultepec Hill, and when Cortés saw it in the following century he wrote that the flow was "as thick as a man's body." Other aqueducts followed.

The eastern part of Lake Texcoco was too salty for chinampa cultivation by now, and that called for a second mighty project: the building of a colossal dike ten miles across the lake from north to south, sealing off Tenochtitlán and its surrounding towns in a fresh-water lagoon. King Nezahualcóyotl of Texcoco, grateful to the Aztecs for restoring him to his throne, supervised the construction of this dike.

The relationship between the cities of Texcoco and Tenochtitlán remained friendly; Texcoco became the Valley's intellectual and artistic center, but real power radiated from the Aztec capital. When Nezahualcóyotl died in 1472, his son Nezahualpilli continued the alliance with the Aztecs.

The gods still demanded sacrifices, and the architects of Aztec power knew that the rapidly built state would collapse unless military adventures continued to maintain the outward thrust. Under Moctezuma I, Aztec soldiers regularly raided the states to the south, carrying away prisoners from the Mixtecs, the Zapotecs, and the Totonacs, successors to the vanished Olmecs. Aztec power now ran from the Gulf Coast to the Pacific. When they turned against the Tarascans in the west, they were met with a shower of copper-tipped arrows and retreated in disarray; another state that more than held its own against them was the eastern one of Tlaxcala, which remained isolated but independent. Nearly all the rest of central Mexico paid tribute to the Aztecs. Under their most successful warrior king, Ahuítzotl (1486–1502), they put together an empire as great as or even greater than that of the Toltecs. It reached to the Guatemalan border, and millions of Mexicans groaned under the burdens imposed by the Aztec tribute collectors. Each year, Tenochtitlán drained from its empire seven thousand tons of corn, four thousand tons each of beans and sage seed, and two million cotton cloaks, plus a mountain of shields, feather headdresses, and war costumes. This immense tribute was employed by the Aztec rulers to pay the countless craftsmen who worked on the constant expansion of Tenochtitlán, already one of the greatest cities of the world.

In Ahuítzotl's reign, 20,000 captives were sacrificed to celebrate the completion of the Great Temple. A new aqueduct was built. Giant pyramids arose. The magnificence of Tenochtitlán was a myth in its own time. It was the commercial center of the empire, and in its markets all commodities could be purchased, using cacao beans, cotton cloaks, or transparent quills filled with gold dust as currency. The Aztec empire had become a complex thing, divided rigidly into social classes with a huge population of commoners, a swarm of serfs, and a small, glittering aristocracy of warriors, priests, and nobles. Atop this social pyramid was the Aztec king, an absolute ruler whose person was divine. Bernardino de Sahagún, a Franciscan priest who arrived in Mexico eight years after the Spanish conquest and did much to collect the traditions of the shattered Aztecs, tells us that "when the ruler went forth, in his hand rested his reed stalk which he set moving in rhythm with his words. His chamberlain and his elders went before him; on both sides, on either hand, they proceeded as they went clearing the way for him. None might cross in front of him; none might come forth before him; none might look up at him; none might come face to face with him."

War was the driving force of this glittering civilization, and sacrifices for the gods were the fruits of war. Aztec savagery has obscured the many greatnesses of this culture; their love of shedding blood has led to frequent unfavorable comparisons with the more placid Mayas and the noble Incas. In fact the Aztecs built a culture as rich as any other, but it is hard to overlook those rivers of blood. Even the art of the Aztecs bristles with ferocity, so that when we study the harsh angles of an Aztec relief we hear the distant boom of drums and the cries of an eager, blood-maddened populace.

At the core of Tenochtitlán was the Sacred Precinct, a paved area surrounding the temple pyramid of Huitzilopochtli and Tlaloc, two of the hungriest of the gods. Other temples nearby were those of Tezcatlipoca, the Toltec death-god, and Xipe Totec, "the Flayed One." The Aztecs had collected all the gods of Mexico and built temples to them all, celebrating the struggle between Quetzalcoatl and Tezcatlipoca, life and death. The effigies of these gods are things of terror; when the great plaza of Mexico City was leveled in 1790 for a government rebuilding project, an idol buried at the time of the conquest appeared, hidden when Mexico City still bore its Aztec name, Tenochtitlán. It was a nightmare figure carved from a block of blue-gray stone, ten feet high, six feet wide and thick, showing a ghastly being with many hands, terrible clawed feet, a girdle of writhing serpents, a face that was no face any earthly creature had ever worn. Yet this was Coatlicue, the mother of the sun-god Huitzilopochtli, a beloved goddess of birth.

That same reconstruction project of 1790 produced another well-known Aztec relic, the Calendar Stone, eleven feet across and intricately inscribed with the mechanisms of the Aztec year. There were eighteen months of twenty days, and each month had its sacred days when blood was fed to Aztec gods. Priests, shaggy and unkempt, their bodies torn by mutilations self-inflicted with agave thorns and the spines of sting rays, mounted the pyramids to the accompaniment of trumpet calls and drums. Incense was burned, the sun gleamed, and the victim came forward, stretching out on the sacrificial stone. The obsidian blade descended and the bleeding heart was held aloft.

The heads of victims crowded the skull racks of the central plaza. Their dripping blood fertilized the earth. Blood and death kept the cycles of the year in motion, and once every fifty-two years all the cycles converged.

This was the time of the New Fire, when old debts were paid, sins were forgiven, and the Aztec world began anew. When darkness fell all fires were extinguished, all utensils broken, all household furnishings destroyed. People huddled within their homes, for spirits were abroad in the darkness. The priests went to the Hill of the Star, outside the city, and rekindled the fire at midnight, holding their breaths for fear that the fire might get out of control and destroy the world, as their annals stated had happened four times in the remote past. The fire was lit, the priests carried it over the causeways into Tenochtitlán, and the new cycle commenced. In the morning, the refuse of the old era was dumped and the people began to refurnish their homes.

These fifty-two-year cycles have provided archeologists with confirmation of the Aztec chronicles. The last New Fire ceremony was held in 1507, and the refuse dump of broken pottery was discovered in 1936 during the construction of a power plant. In the upper levels lay Aztec ware that showed Spanish influence in its glazed surfaces and European design, but below was a layer of earlier type, the pottery of the fifty-two-year period from 1455 to 1507. Then, at Texcoco, the dump of the previous cycle, 1403–1455, was uncovered, corresponding to the period of alliance between the Aztecs and the Texcoco people. The 1351–1403 cycle is represented poorly, but the 1299–1351 style is found chiefly at Colhuacán, supporting the traditional tale of Aztec serfdom there.

The ceremony of 1507, the last ever held, was presided over by the ninth Aztec king, the tragic Moctezuma II. (His name was mysteriously corrupted to Montezuma by some writers.) He had come to the throne in 1502, succeeding the militarist Ahuítzotl. He was a brooding, reflective man, obsessed by the legend of Quetzalcoatl's return, and when the omens began to hint at a time of upheaval, Moctezuma knew that his day was ending. His brother-in-law Nezahualpilli, king of Texcoco, reading the omens also, predicted the destruction of Mexico.

The Spanish had made their way through the islands of the Caribbean and had planted their first settlements in South and Central America, but Mexico escaped their attention until 1511. A shipwreck dumped some Spaniards on the coast of Yucatán then, and the two survivors were enslaved by the Mayas. Three years later, there were colonists in Panama, and in 1518 came the reconnaissance trip of Juan de Grijalva, who landed near modern Veracruz. Moctezuma took this as the harbinger of Quetzalcoatl's second coming.

Tempted by Mexican gold, the Spaniards returned in force in 1519 under Hernando Cortés. He scouted the Yucatán coast, landed at Tabasco in March, and quickly established his supremacy over the Indians of the coastal country. They showered darts

and arrows at him as though they did not know he was Quetzalcoatl; the Spaniards replied with the blaze of harquebuses. The
flash of gunpowder drew screams of fear from the Indians. Their
quilted cotton armor was little protection. The first battles were
the last. Tabasco surrendered, told Cortés of the golden city of
Tenochtitlán somewhere in the west, and presented him with his
most useful asset: a slave girl named Malinal, or Malinche, who
spoke many languages.

Cortés had already rescued from the Mayas the Spaniard Guerrero, of the 1511 shipwreck. He spoke Mayan, and so did Malinal. Guerrero taught her Spanish. She was baptized a Christian
and served as Cortés' interpreter and public-relations agent as
he led his army inland, burning his ships behind him.

From Moctezuma came more ambassadors to study these
bearded strangers. One of them was practically Cortés' twin in
features and physique, which startled the Spaniards. Moctezuma
sent lavish gifts. Bernal Díaz, one of the many Spanish historians who left eyewitness accounts of the conquest, describes them:

The first article presented was a wheel like a sun, as big as a cart-
wheel, with many sorts of pictures on it, the whole of fine gold, and
a wonderful thing to behold. . . . . Then another wheel was presented of greater size made of silver of great brilliance in imitation
of the moon with other figures on it. . . . Then were brought
twenty golden ducks, beautifully worked and very natural looking,
and some ornaments like dogs, and many articles of gold worked in
the shape of tigers and lions and monkeys, and ten collars beautifully
worked and other necklaces; and twelve arrows and a bow with its
string, and two rods like staffs of justice, five palms long, all in
beautiful hollow work of fine gold. Then there were presented crests
of gold and plumes of rich green feathers . . . over thirty loads of
beautiful cotton cloth . . . and so many other things were there that
it is useless my trying to describe them.

Cortés gave each ambassador two shirts and some blue glass
beads and requested an audience with Moctezuma in his capital.
They returned to Tenochtitlán, and came back with still more
gifts, but politely informed the Spaniards that Moctezuma had
no wish to see them in person.

With the Aztec ambassadors, Cortés entered the territory of the Totonacs, who forever were on the verge of rebellion against Tenochtitlán. Cortés quietly told the Totonacs he would support them if they revolted, and he told the Aztec emissaries he would help to quell any Totonac uprising. And then it was onward toward the Valley of Mexico, while Moctezuma's ambassadors, not knowing if they were dealing with a god or an invader, tried to find some way to make him turn back.

At the stoutly independent city-state of Tlaxcala, Cortés ran into difficulties that not even Malinal, that shrewd diplomat and interpreter, could rescue him from. Here, early in September, 1519, Cortés became embroiled in battle. "How they began to charge on us!" exclaimed Bernal Díaz. "What a hail of stones sped from their slings! As for their bowmen, the javelins lay like corn on the threshing floor; all of them barbed and fire-hardened, which would pierce any armor and would reach the vitals where there is no protection. . . . How they pressed on us and with what valor and what mighty shouts and yells they charged upon us!" There were three battles with the Tlaxcalans. Then Malinal—or Doña Marina, as the Spaniards called her— negotiated a peace just when Cortés' men were all for a quick retreat to the coast. She did more than that: she told the Tlaxcalan chiefs that Cortés had come to destroy the Aztecs. Nothing could have pleased Tlaxcala more, and abruptly the Spaniards acquired fiercely loyal allies.

Accompanied by Tlaxcalans, Cortés proceeded to Cholula, an Aztec subject state. He left the Tlaxcalans outside the city and tried more diplomacy, but when he discovered a real or fancied plot against his life he brought his Indian warriors into the town, and the Cholulans were massacred. Of course, Moctezuma got full reports. But he could not lift his hand against the man he believed was Quetzalcoatl, and he remained in a kind of paralysis even as the Spaniards marched right into Tenochtitlán.

They got their first glimpse of the Aztec capital on November 8, 1519. They had never seen a city like this. Barcelona could not equal it, nor Madrid, nor Toledo. "During the morning," Bernal Díaz declares, we arrived at a broad causeway and continued our march toward Iztapalapa, and when we saw so many cities and villages built in the water and other great towns on dry land and that straight and level causeway going towards Mexico [Tenochtitlán], we were amazed and said that it was like the enchantments they tell of in the legend of Amadis, on account of the great towers and cues and buildings rising from the water, and all built of masonry. And some of our soldiers asked whether the things that we saw were not a dream.

Tenochtitlán was the hub of an empire whose population was twice as great as Spain's. Cortés and his few hundred Spaniards gasped at the three huge causeways, the twenty square miles of the city with its Venice-like canals, the gardens and temples, the pyramids, the palaces. The Aztecs were interested in the strangers, too. They had never seen horses before, nor men with white skins (and one of the grooms was a Negro, also a strange sight in Mexico). Moctezuma himself came out on a litter to greet them and made them welcome, quartering them in the palace of his father.

Francisco López de Gómara, Cortés' secretary and one of the most reliable chroniclers of the expedition, describes Moctezuma as "a man of middling size, thin, and, like all Indians, of a very dark complexion. He wore his hair long and had no more than six bristles on his chin, black and about an inch long. He was of an amiable though severe disposition, affable, well-spoken, and gracious, which made him respected and feared." Gómara writes rhapsodically of Moctezuma's private zoo, with its "lions," lynxes, falcons, and crocodiles, of his lovely pleasure gardens, and of incredible Tenochtitlán itself. Moctezuma took the Spaniards to see the Great Temple, which to Gómara "resembled a pyramid of Egypt, save that it did not end in a point, but in a square platform eight or ten fathoms wide." A Spaniard named Gonzalo de Umbria counted the skulls in the sacred bone heap and found 136,000.

After six days of tourism, Cortés decided that he had seen enough of Tenochtitlán, and the time for action had come. With thirty men carrying concealed weapons he went to Moctezuma, chatted pleasantly with him for a while, then accused him of plotting treachery and announced that the king was under arrest.

Moctezuma was understandably shaken. "My person is not such as can be taken prisoner, and, even if I should consent to it, my people would not suffer it," he declared. But after four hours of discussion he went off voluntarily to the palace where the Spaniards resided. Cortés, with his 450 men, had captured Moctezuma in the heart of Tenochtitlán without lifting a hand.

Moctezuma accepted his fate with strange resignation and told his people that all was well. From his quarters among the Spaniards he conducted the business of state. He swore fealty to King Carlos of Spain and assembled some millions of dollars' worth of golden ornaments as a present for his unseen overlord. Cortés must have felt he was living a dream.

A cold awakening came. In the spring of 1520, just when all was going so well at Tenochtitlán, a second force of Spaniards put ashore near modern Veracruz under the arrogant Pánfilo de Narváez. They had not come to reinforce Cortés but to steal Mexico from him. With half his own men, and several thousand Indian allies, Cortés hastened to the coast, putting his handsome blond lieutenant Pedro de Alvarado in charge at Tenochtitlán.

Alvarado was the sort of conquistador that Spain has been trying to live down for four hundred years. While Cortés was away trouncing Narváez, Alvarado embarked on a massacre of Aztecs during a religious festival. Their dreamlike self-restraint exploded at last, and Cortés returned to the capital to find his garrison under fierce attack.

At Doña Marina's urgings, Moctezuma reluctantly tried to calm his people, and he appeared on the roof of his palace prison. He spoke briefly; the Aztecs responded with a shower of stones and darts, apparently aimed not at him but at the Spaniards who guarded him. They stepped aside, exposing Moctezuma to the fatal barrage. Cortés was appalled, not only because he had genuinely admired Moctezuma but because he knew that the dead king had been his only hope of restoring order in Tenochtitlán. Now there was nothing to do but engineer a retreat to the friendly city of Tlaxcala.

The retreat was carried out under frightful attack. The Spaniards ever after referred to that night as *la Noche Triste*, the Night of Sorrow. Cortés had added to his own 450 men about a thousand of Narváez' men, but during the retreat hundreds of the Spaniards were killed, and thousands of their Indian allies. "Who, indeed, would not weep at the death and ruin of those who had entered in such triumph, pomp, and rejoicing?" Gómara wrote. "If the retreat had occurred in daylight perhaps fewer would have died and there would have been less confusion, but, since it happened in the night and in the fog, it was an affair of many shouts, wailing, howling, and frightfulness, as the victorious Indians invoked their gods, insulted the fallen, and killed those who defended themselves."

It was the greatest moment of the Aztec resistance. Based now at Tlaxcala, Cortés spent the next year gathering support for his real war against the Aztecs. The first conquest had been but a dream after all. His campaign was eased by the general hatred that the non-Aztec states felt for the lords of Tenochtitlán; heedless of their own futures, the Totonacs and the Tlaxcalans and even the people of Texcoco rallied to Cortés' standard. Texcoco was the command point from which Cortés closed in on Tenochtitlán. Hundreds of thousands of natives besieged the great capital and burst into it.

The new king was Cuauhtémoc, Moctezuma's nephew and to this day a Mexican national hero. He vowed unending defiance, leading a bitter defense, giving ground from street to street in a battle that lasted eighty-five days and cost 117,000 Aztec lives. The conflict ended on August 13, 1521. The starving Aztec survivors surrendered at last, and amid the reek of death Cortés accepted Cuauhtémoc's submission with all military honors. He remained a prisoner for three years before Cortés found reason to have him hanged.

Mexico became a Spanish dominion. Priests of Jesus appeared to destroy the idols and spread the gospel. Many chroniclers recorded the customs of the Indian cultures even as they were being eradicated.

Mexico was conquered and yet not conquered. The Tlaxcalans were allowed to keep their land as a reward for their services. The Mixtecs and Zapotecs went on as before. Spanish culture became a thin overlay concealing but not obliterating the Indian heritage. The glitter of the Aztec world was trampled underfoot, and no resurgence of that greatness would appear, but the customs of the simpler folk endured and endure. It is an inward heritage now. Only five Mexicans out of each hundred have no Indian blood in their veins. Forty out of each hundred are full-blooded descendants of the defeated race. And the old memories remain. Cortés is reviled and Cuauhtémoc exalted. Throughout the land archeologists, many of them great-great-great-grandchildren of the conquerors or of the conquered, labor to recover that bright world of the past. "All through the Colonial era and even up to now," writes the archeologist George Vaillant, "the northern district of Mexico [City] has found favor neither as a residential quarter nor as a business center. Today there are railroad yards and slums where the Aztec civilization bled to death. The ghosts of its heroic defenders still haunt the place."

Six

Easter Island: "Talking Boards" And Giant Heads

A lonely, barren island of volcanic rock, a thousand miles from anywhere, has been tantalizing scientists with its mysteries since its discovery by Dutch sailors almost two hundred fifty years ago. Bleak and forlorn, alone amid a million square miles of empty ocean, Easter Island was the dwelling place of a people whose brooding stone statues are masterpieces of art and whose strange hieroglyphic writing, unique among the island cultures of the Pacific, has kept scholars in hot debate for a century.

The island itself seems an insignificant home for such a fascinating culture. It is a mere sixty-four square miles in area, a three-sided wedge of rock without a single good harbor. Its cliff-lined shores seem ominous and forbidding. Jagged reefs of volcanic lava rim the island; the sea batters remorselessly against them, nibbling away at the coast from year to year, chewing at it in showers of white spume. Offshore, the waters drop rapidly to a depth of 10,000 feet. The closest land is Pitcairn Island, where the *Bounty* mutineers landed after setting Captain Bligh adrift. Pitcairn is 1,100 miles to the west of Easter Island. And to the east, some 2,300 miles away, is the coast of Chile. Easter Island is one of the most isolated places in the world.

A British buccaneer named Edward Davis may have been the first European to sight Easter Island. He went that way in 1687 but turned away without attempting a landing, after having spotted a sandy beach and high mountains. Geographers who read his narrative thought he had seen the shores of a new continent, for new continents in the Pacific were just then the object of high interest. Many seamen were looking for them, hoping to repeat Columbus' feat and stumble onto a New World. So the ridge of land Davis thought he saw was given the name of "Davis Land," and navigators searched in vain for the continent that was not there.

In the next century the myth of Davis Land was exploded. The Dutch admiral Jacob Roggeveen, aboard the *Arena,* came to this isolated outpost and landed there on Easter Sunday, 1722. To commemorate the date of his landfall, he gave the island the name it bears today. (He did not know, and probably did not care, that the island already had several native names of its own, of which the most interesting is *Te Pito-te-Henua,* "Navel of the World.")

Roggeveen was fascinated by the island. He noted in his log that the people "are big in stature, and their natural hue is not black, but pale yellow or sallowish." In their ears they wore round or oval plugs of silver, or so Roggeveen thought, three inches long and two inches in diameter. (Actually the earplugs were made of bone.)

The ears of the Easter Islanders startled the Dutch sailors; one noted in his journal that "their ears were so long that they hung down as far as to the shoulders." Those with the longest ears appeared to be priests, distinguished from the others "not only by their wearing great white plugs in their ear lobes, but in having the head wholly shaven and hairless." If there had been an anthropologist on board, he would certainly have remarked on the similarity of the islander's ears to those of the Incas of Peru, who also stretched their lobes with inserted plugs. But Peru was thousands of miles to the east across a trackless ocean, and the Incas had been crushed a century and a half before, and Roggeveen was carrying no anthropologists in his crew.

Still, he had an anthropologist's eye for customs. "What the form of worship of these people comprises," Roggeveen wrote, "we were not able to gather any full knowledge of, owing to the shortness of our stay among them; we noticed only that they kindle fire in front of certain remarkably tall stone figures they set up; and, thereafter squatting on their heels with heads bowed down, they bring the palms of their hands together and alternately raise and lower them."

The stone figures "caused us to be filled with wonder, for we could not understand how it was possible that people who are destitute of heavy or thick timber, and also of stout cordage, out of which to construct gear, had been able to erect them. . . . Some of these statues were a good 30 feet high and broad in proportion." Roggeveen claimed that close inspection showed the statues to be made of clay covered with a veneer of stone, which he said explained how the natives had been able to move such huge structures about, but no later visitor to Easter Island has ever made the same observation.

The Dutch visit ended tragically. Some of Roggeveen's crewmen, mistaking the natives' gestures of friendship for menacing expressions, panicked and opened fire. A dozen Easter Islanders were killed and many more wounded—the first, but not the last, of the white man's crimes against these people.

After Roggeveen, no ship called at Easter Island for half a century. Then Spanish explorers under Captain Felipe González stopped there in 1770, and, unaware of Roggeveen's visit, annexed the island to Spain, calling it San Carlos. González was impressed with the "tall, well built" natives, commenting that they looked more like Europeans than Indians. He noted in his journal, "I believe, from their docility and intelligence, that it would be easy to domesticate them and to convert them to any religion which might be put before them."

González, too, gasped at the great stone statues, with their long ears and sightless eyes and somber, thin-lipped faces. In words similar to Roggeveen's he wondered how a people lacking iron, hemp, and stout timber could have carved and erected such works, which he found mounted on stone platforms and topped with "caps" of a different kind of stone, reddish in color. Before he left, the Spaniard caused his annexation of the island to be set forth in an official proclamation which was read to the islanders. He invited the bewildered chiefs to sign the document, and they did so willingly enough. Some of the chieftains made scrawled scribbles in imitation of the Spanish signatures—but several, to quote González, "signed or attested the official document by marking upon it certain characters in their own form of script." One drew the outlined figure of a bird. It was the first time that white men had seen an Easter Island hieroglyph, one of the characters that later would pose an even greater scientific mystery than the statues. But González and his men had no idea of that.

Four years after González, the great English seafarer Captain James Cook visited Easter Island. A change had come over it since Roggeveen's day. The Dutchman had described the island as green and fertile, but Cook found it parched and dreary, with few plantations. The imposing statues, too, had suffered; many had toppled and broken. It was as though some civil war had swept the island, leaving it in ruins.

Cook's accounts of his voyages were best-sellers of their time, published and pirated throughout Europe, and soon many people were eagerly discussing the island of the strange stone statues. Other explorers made it a point to stop there. Some came out of greed rather than curiosity. In 1808, an American ship, the *Nancy*, kipnapped twenty-two Easter Islanders to be sold as slaves. Other slave raids followed, bringing disease and suffering in their wake.

The worst crime against the Easter Islanders was committed in 1862. A flotilla of Peruvian slavers arrived and carried off a thousand men to work mining guano off the South American coast. Nearly all died within a few months. A scant fifteen were finally returned to their homes, bringing with them the germs of tuberculosis and smallpox. Epidemics finished the job of decimating Easter Island. A population that had numbered some 4,000 when Roggeveen landed in 1722 dwindled to a pitiful 111 by 1877.

The great days of the statue builders were over by then, and the islanders moved like phantoms among the relics of their mighty past. In 1888, Chile annexed the tortured island and brought a measure of peace to it. Its population has grown until today there are about 1,100 Easter Islanders. There is little disease on Easter Island now. Many of the natives work in the Chilean-operated sheep farm that is the island's only major industry, and the rest support themselves by carving wooden statuettes to be sold as curios.

The Easter Island statues continued to enthrall the world in the nineteenth century, and theories of their origin multiplied endlessly. More than six hundred of the statues, some as big as a four-story house, were scattered like vast dolls over the island. Their beauty and strangeness appealed irresistibly to the romantic imagination. When the first modern scientific expedition set out for Easter Island in 1914, investigating the statues was one of its chief aims.

That expedition itself now seems like something out of a forgotten epoch. Its leaders were Mrs. Katherine Routledge, an English anthropologist, and her husband Scoresby—intelligent, curious-minded people of private means who were interested enough in Easter Island to underwrite the costs of their own expedition. We know that Mrs. Routledge speaks from a vanished world when we come upon sentences like this in her book, *The Mystery of Easter Island,* published in 1919: "It was therefore decided, as Scoresby is a keen yachtsman, that it was worth while to procure in England a little ship of our own, adapted to the purpose, and to sail out in her. As the Panama Canal was not open, and the route by Suez would be longer, the way would lie through the Magellan Straits."

The Routledge expedition arrived at Easter Island at dawn on March 29, 1914, and dropped anchor at Cook's Bay. Mrs. Routledge soon attempted to get some information from the natives about the giant statues. "The present natives take little interest in the remains," she wrote.

The statues are to them facts of every-day life in much the same way as stones or banana-trees. "Have you no *moai"* (as they are termed) "in England?" was asked by one boy, in a tone in which surprise was slightly mingled with contempt. . . . The information given in reply to questions is generally wildly mythical, and any real knowledge crops up only indirectly.

She found that the statues were incorporated into burial platforms called *ahu.* There were some two hundred and sixty of these, mostly near the coast, at intervals of a few hundred yards all around the island. The Routledges sketched and measured each one, aided by old Easter Islanders who supplied names and traditions from memory or imagination. "A typical image *ahu,"* Mrs. Routledge wrote, is composed of a long wall running parallel with the sea, which, in a large specimen, is as much as 15 feet in height and 300 feet in length; it is buttressed on the land side with a great slope of masonry. The wall is in three divisions. The main or central portion projects in the form of a terrace on which the images stood, with their backs to the sea; it is therefore broad enough to carry their oval bed-plates; these measure up to about 10 feet in length by 8 feet or 9 feet in width, and are flush with the wall. On the great *ahu* of Tongariki there have been fifteen statues, but sometimes an *ahu* has carried one figure only.

The stone statues had originally risen with their backs to the sea on these immense platforms, and the bodies of the dead were placed before them, wrapped in blankets and reeds, for mourning periods of several years. After that the bones were carried to a vault elsewhere or sometimes left on the *ahu,* and the end of the mourning was marked by a great feast, after which, as one informant told the Routledges, "Papa was finished." Mrs. Routledge compared the *ahu* to

a vast theatre stage, of which the floor runs gradually upwards from the footlights. The back of the stage, which is thus the highest part, is occupied by a great terrace, on which are set up in line the giant images, each one well separated from his neighbor, and all facing the spectator. Irrespective of where he stands he will ever see them towering above him, clear cut out against a turquoise sky.

This was the way Roggeveen had seen the statues, but by the time of Cook's arrival nearly all had been overthrown, and the Routledges could not find any Easter Islanders who remembered when a statue had been standing. The oldest men had traditional tales to tell of civil wars during which one statue after another had been thrown down. The *ahu* themselves had suffered from the beating of the waves against the shore; in many places the coast had been eroded, dumping *ahu* and fallen statues into the sea.

The Routledges visited the quarries where the statues had been cut. They were located along the slope of a mountain of compressed volcanic ash. About two hundred feet up the grassy hillside, the reddish-brown rock of the mountain had been cut into a series of ledges and chambers, and here were statues in all stages of completion. This quarry has been a center of study for every succeeding expedition to Easter Island. When Alfred Métraux of the Musée de l'Homme in Paris led a Belgian-French group there in 1934, he found that

there are few spectacles in the world more impressive than the sight of the statue quarry on the slopes of Ranoraraku. The place is indeed sinister. Imagine a half-crumbled volcano, a black shore line, and huge cliffs which rise up from the sea with smooth green pastures above them. Guarding the quarry, near the volcano, is an army of giant stone figures scattered in the most picturesque disorder. Most of them still stand out boldly. Successive landslides have partially covered others, so that only their heads emerge from the ground, like those of a cursed race buried alive in quicksand. Behind the rows of the erect statues, along the slopes of the volcano, there are 150 figures still in the process of being born. Wherever one looks in the quarry, one sees half-finished sculpture. Ledges of the mountains have been given human shape. Caves have been opened in which statues rest like those on medieval sepulchres in the crypt of some great cathedral. Hardly a single surface has been left uncarved by the artists in their frenzy to exploit the soft tufa [volcanic rock] of the mountain.

The quarry gives an inescapable impression that the work was suddenly interrupted. Métraux wrote:

There is something weird in the sight of this deserted workshop with the dead giants all about. At every step, one stumbles over discarded stone hammers. It is as if the quarry had been abandoned on the eve of some holiday, and the workers were expecting on the day after to return and resume their tasks; indeed, in several cases, only a few more blows would have been needed to cut the statues finally free from the rock of the slope.

And Mrs. Routledge recorded the local tradition that a certain old woman who lived near the slope was cook to the image makers and also had the power to move the statues about at will. One day the quarriers caught a fine lobster while she was elsewhere and ate it before she returned. When she discovered the remains of the lobster and saw how she had been neglected, she became so angry that she caused all the images to fall down, and the work was halted forever.

How these great statues were carved and transported was the

big question, of course. Roggeveen had been the first to pose it, in 1722, and had answered it to his own, if no one else's, satisfaction by inventing the notion that the statues were made of wads of clay covered by a thin layer of stone. Later explorers guessed at weights of 500 tons or more. Mrs. Routledge estimated that the biggest ones weighed 40 or 50 tons, but Métraux, twenty years later, showed that most of them weighed 5 or 6 tons, with only a few as heavy as 30 tons.

Even five tons is a substantial weight to drag about, particularly on an island lacking timber and cordage for sledges. Mrs. Routledge suggested that rollers were used, but she put the idea forth hesitantly. Métraux believed that the statues were hauled on skids made of sea-borne driftwood and pulled by ropes made from the fibers of the paper mulberry. More detailed studies were carried out by the Norwegian adventurer-archeologist Thor Heyerdahl during his expedition to Easter Island in 1955–56.

Heyerdahl actually got the modern islanders to re-enact the old methods of moving the statues, thus testing the traditional techniques in the most practical way. He reported that the polished statues were packed in tough reeds, to protect them on the journey from the quarries to the *ahu,* and then were placed in a large sledgelike frame:

A recent experiment undertaken on the island shows that 180 natives suffice to pull a twelve-ton statue across the terrain by means of ropes and wooden skids. From 500 to 700 natives would be able to transport even the larger statues the same way, and there is reason to suspect that the transport was facilitated by piecemeal jerks on ropes passing through stout wooden shears placed across the neck of the statue. This would lever it along in a seesaw motion on the fulcrum of its bulging stomach, a method which would considerably reduce the manpower needed.

When the statue reached the place where it was to stand, it was maneuvered upright with much the same combination of leverage and muscle power that the ancient Egyptians employed in building their pyramids. Heyerdahl found that the islanders used wooden levers to lift the statues a short distance from the ground on one side, jamming in small stones as supports before repeating the process on the other side. In this way, the still-horizontal statue rose on a pile of stones until it was level with the top of the *ahu.* Then, according to Heyerdahl's researches,

Simultaneous levering operations on each side of the head and shoulder section were started, and the same process of inserting smaller and bigger stones began to raise the head above the level of the feet, until the giant reached an angle of more than 45 degrees from the horizontal. Stays were now lashed to the statue to prevent it from toppling over, and the underbuilding continued until the final and most critical moment when the pulling of ropes caused the giant to tip into a vertical position with its flat body base resting on top of a large slab built into the surface platform of the *ahu.*

Heyerdahl put a dozen islanders to work and found that they could raise and erect a 25-ton statue in eighteen days, using two wooden levers and a great many small stones. He also persuaded Pedro Atan, the mayor of the island, to lead a team of six men in a stone-cutting experiment. For three days they chopped away at the quarry. Heyerdahl calculated on this basis that it would have taken six men twelve months to finish a statue 15 to 20 feet long. The tools that they used were hand picks flaked out of a hard stone called andesite.

No longer is there much mystery about the stone heads of Easter Island. The real enigmas of the place lie elsewhere. Perhaps the greatest puzzle of all is the "writing" of the Islanders, the so-called "talking boards."

In 1864 a Catholic missionary, Brother Eugène Eyraud, came to Easter Island. He noticed certain tablets and staves covered with rows of carved symbols. These were found in many Easter Island houses, but no one attached any particular importance to them or knew what they were. Brother Eyraud, apparently regarding the symbols on the boards as the texts of pagan prayers, encouraged the natives to destroy them.

But a few survived and made their way to Tepano Jaussen, Bishop of Tahiti. Bishop Jaussen examined the sticks and boards, saw that they were covered with carefully carved and attractive figures of equal height, and came to the conclusion that they represented some form of native writing. He ordered that all of the inscribed boards be collected and preserved for study, but by this time most of them had been used as firewood or to repair leaky canoes. Less than two dozen survived. Today they are scattered in museums all over the world, with the bulk of the collection in Belgium.

Bishop Jaussen plunged into an extensive study of the Easter Island tablets. He knew how important they were, if they truly represented writing. No other kind of writing had ever been found in any South Sea island. The tablets were unique. But did the symbols really represent writing, or were they just a form of ornamental decoration? Scholars have been arguing over that point since Bishop Jaussen's time. Only a few years ago, Professor I. J. Gelb, who played an important role in the decipherment of the Hittite hieroglyphics of Syria and Asia Minor, insisted that the Easter Island inscriptions were "not even writing in the most primitive sense of the word . . . they probably represent nothing else but pictorial concoctions for magical purposes."

Bishop Jaussen thought otherwise. He identified hundreds of different signs, a third of an inch to half an inch long, showing "surprising elegance and beauty—precise and complex in detail yet boldly drawn." The symbols, which had been cut with sharks' teeth or with gravers made from the volcanic glass obsidian, depicted human beings, fish, plants, birds, turtles, and curious abstract geometrical forms. They were inscribed on flat boards of irregular shape, and just about every square inch of space on the tablets was utilized, with rows of symbols running lengthwise on both sides of the boards.

The native name for the boards was *kohau rongorongo. Kohau* meant "staff" or "stick"; a *rongorongo* was a specially trained chanter whose function it was to recite sacred hymns at festivals. *Kohau rongorongo,* then, could best be translated as "talking boards."

Father Zumbohn of the Easter Island mission was the first to try to decipher the tablets. He sent for a few learned natives and showed them the boards. They looked at the symbols and immediately began to chant a hymn, but after a while they started to disagree over the text, loudly telling one another, "No, it doesn't go like that!" Father Zumbohn was discouraged by the debate and gave up his attempt.

On Tahiti, meanwhile, Bishop Jaussen had found an emigrant

from Easter Island who claimed to have been trained in his youth as a *rongorongo* man, a professional chanter. The Bishop summoned this man, whose name was Metoro, and gave him a tablet to read.

Metoro picked up the tablet, studied it a moment, turned it this way and that. Then he burst into a Polynesian chant. He "read" from left to right along one row, then came back from right to left along the next row. This confirmed Bishop Jaussen's guess that the Easter Island hieroglyphics were written *boustrophedon,* a Greek word meaning "as one leads the oxen when plowing"—that is, up one row and back down the next. Metoro did not bother to turn the tablet upside down when reading the right-to-left row, although the characters in it were obviously inverted relative to the adjoining left-to-right row.

As Metoro chanted, the Bishop jotted down the words of the Polynesian songs. Later, he translated the text into French. But what he had written down was jumbled and all but incoherent. Perplexed, the Bishop tried to compile a "dictionary" of the Easter Island symbols but finally declared in despair, "One has to resign, there is no sense in it."

The Easter Island script became a football for philologists. It was generally agreed that Metoro had merely been fooling the poor Bishop, pretending to "read" the tablets he was shown but actually doing no more than inventing nonsense as he went along. The experience of a man named Croft supported this idea. Croft, an American living on Tahiti, met another Easter Island emigré who claimed to understand the tablets. One Sunday, Croft showed him a photograph of one of the Bishop's "talking boards." The native responded with a chant, which Croft took down. But the American lost his notes, and the following week he asked the native to return to repeat the reading. Again the islander recited, and again Croft transcribed what he heard; but the chant seemed different this time. A week later, Croft had the islander read the tablet for him a third time.

By now Croft had found his first page of notes, and he was able to see that the three texts were wholly different from one another. The native had not been reading at all, merely chanting the first hymns that came into his mind. Evidently Bishop

Jaussen's informant Metoro had been doing the same thing.

Research continued. In 1882, a German warship stopped at Easter Island for three and a half days and collected information about the tablets on behalf of scholars in Berlin. Four years later, a vessel of the United States Navy, the U.S.S. *Mohican*, called at Easter Island, and its paymaster W. J. Thomson, was able to obtain two superb tablets which are now in the National Museum, Washington, D.C.—the only "talking boards" in American hands. But no one made any headway toward solving the problem of the inscriptions.

When the Scoresby Routledge expedition reached Easter Island in 1914, one of Mrs. Routledge's aims was to find a native who could translate the boards or at least help her to understand the part they had played in the old culture of the island. But that old culture had disintegrated; the island's past was a closed book to the few survivors who lived there. The only Easter Islander who as much as claimed to know anything about the boards was an old man named Tomenika, who was on his deathbed when the expedition arrived.

Mrs. Routledge's conversations with Tomenika had to be carried on through a doorway, for she could not enter the hut in which the old man lay dying of leprosy. He tried to give her some information, but his rambling, vague answers only compounded the mystification. "Every way that could be thought of was tried to elicit information, but without real success," Mrs. Routledge wrote.

He did draw two fresh symbols, saying first they were "new" and then "old," and stating they represented the man who gave the *koro* [a feast] but "there was no sign meaning a man." . . . The answers, on the whole, were so wandering and contradictory, that after a second visit under those conditions, making five in all, the prospect of getting anything further of material value did not seem to justify the risks to others, however slight.

As she left the hut a last time, she hesitated, searching her mind for some question that the old man might be able to answer, some way to get at the information he so dimly remembered. Then she departed.

[150]

It was late afternoon on a day of unusual calm, everything in the lonely spot was perfectly still, the sea lay below like a sheet of glass, the sun as a globe of fire was nearing the horizon, while close at hand lay the old man gradually sinking, and carrying in his tired brain the last remnants of a once-prized knowledge. In a fortnight he was dead.

There was no hope of getting information about the tablets from any of the other islanders. Would it be possible, then, to decipher them?

There are different degrees of difficulty in tackling an unknown form of writing. In some cases, the script itself is understood, but the language cannot be translated. This is the situation with the Etruscan inscriptions found in Italy; the Etruscans used the same alphabet as the ancient Romans, and we can "read" their inscriptions—but the words make no sense to us.

Sometimes the underlying language is known, but the script is a mystery. The decipherer can crack such a puzzle if he finds an inscription in the unknown script parallel to an identically worded inscription in a known form of writing. Thus Jean François Champollion, who penetrated the secret of Egyptian hieroglyphics 150 years ago, was able to achieve success because he had the famous Rosetta stone, a text written both in hieroglyphics and in classical Greek. It is even possible—using modern code-solving techniques—to decipher a text of known language but unknown script without the use of a bilingual inscription. Hans Bauer did just this when he decoded the cuneiform alphabet of Ras Shamra in 1930. More recently, the trick was turned by the late Michael Ventris in his astonishing decipherment of the Linear B writing of ancient Crete, which he proved to be an early form of the Greek language written with non-Grecian characters.

Most puzzling of all is the case where both the script and the language are unknown. As one expert put it, "Nothing can be made out of nothing." The best example of such a mystery, perhaps, is the writing of the Indus Valley civilization, a city-building people who created a complex culture in India more than four thousand years ago. We have no clue to the nature of the Indus Valley language nor any way of interpreting the hieroglyphic script found in the ruins of the ancient Indus cities of Mohenjo-Daro and Harappa, so those inscriptions remain incomprehensible today, decades after they were first discovered.

The Easter Island tablets did not pose so forbidding a challenge. If their characters were writing at all, and not just decoration, then they were almost certainly written in the Polynesian language which, in various dialects, is spoken all over the South Pacific. Although, as we will see, there is loud controversy about the ancient inhabitants of Easter Island, no one disagrees with the belief that the island's population was of Polynesian stock at the time the "talking boards" were carved. The trick was to coax some meaning out of the intricately carved symbols by matching them to known Polynesian words.

There were theories galore. In the 1930's, a Hungarian linguist named Wilhelm von Hevesy pointed out amazing similarities between certain Easter Island hieroglyphics and those of the Indus Valley civilization. He found some fifty symbols that were almost identical in the two scripts. Some speculative thinkers, willing to leap to the broadest of conclusions on the basis of the narrowest of evidence, decided that the Easter Islanders must be refugees from India who had spread through the Pacific after the downfall of Mohenjo-Daro and Harappa. But there were many symbols in the two scripts that could not be matched at all. The strongest argument against Hevesy's idea was the fact that the Indus civilization had vanished without a trace about 1500 B.C., while the earliest known settlements on Easter Island dated from about A.D. 400. The inscribed boards that have survived, furthermore, must have been carved in the last century or two. Despite the gap of two or three thousand years, Hevesy insisted that the whole Polynesian culture—of which Easter Island was the easternmost outpost—had originated in India more than forty centuries ago.

All we can say of this theory, as of now, is that it is not proven and not likely to be proven. Most authorities think that the resemblance between Indus and Easter Island writing is pure coincidence, though a startling one.

In 1938, the Austrian anthropologist Robert Heine-Geldern proposed a different hypothesis. He saw resemblances between the Easter Island hieroglyphics and certain Chinese characters of the Shang Dynasty, dating from 1500 B.C.! Ten symbols, according to Heine-Geldern, were common not only to China and Easter Island but also to the Indus Valley. This theory had the advantage of explaining the settlement of the Pacific islands and also dealing with the troublesome matter of the origin of Shang. Heine-Geldern drew an awesome picture of an advanced Asiatic people building the great cities of the Indus Valley, radiating eastward to found the kingdom of Shang, and eventually reaching the islands of the Pacific.

This, too, is still in the realm of the unproven. Heine-Geldern's imposing scheme of cultural migration has its admirers, but it stands on a flimsy foundation of ten similar characters in three different scripts that span thousands of years in time.

There were dozens of other interpretations. One scholar saw a link between the hieroglyphics of Easter Island and those of ancient Egypt. Another found a connection between the Easter Island script and certain embroidered patterns from the Indonesian island of Sumatra. Yet another claimed to discern a relationship between Easter Island writing and a form of picture writing in use among a tribe of South American Indians. Many of these theories bordered on the fantastic or jumped headlong into pure fantasy.

A note of reality returned in 1953, when a thirty-year-old German named Thomas S. Barthel began to study the "talking boards" of Easter Island. Barthel had served as a cryptographer in World War II, helping to crack military codes. After the war, he became interested in the decipherment of unknown scripts. He first worked on the Mayan writing of Mexico but soon shifted to the Easter Island problem. Barthel made a thorough study of Polynesian cultures to prepare himself for his task.

Then, working at Hamburg University, he contacted museums all over the world, from Russia to Hawaii, asking for copies, photographs, or plaster casts of Easter Island inscriptions. Eventually Barthel had 12,000 signs to work with. Through tedious analysis, he found that there were about 120 basic signs, combined in various ways to form some 1,000 different characters.

This told him at once that the Easter Island writing could not be an alphabet, a script in which each symbol stands for a distinct sound. Thirty or forty characters are enough to comprise an alphabet that includes each basic sound. No, the Easter Island symbols had to stand for whole syllables or even for complete words.

How to break the code?

Barthel went right back to the beginning of the study of the "talking boards," to Bishop Jaussen and Metoro. Most later investigators had written Metoro off as a fraud and Bishop Jaussen's notes as worthless. Barthel was not so sure. He searched for the Bishop's original notebooks—but it appeared that they had vanished.

The quest took the young cryptographer from Tahiti to France, then to Belgium, and finally to a monastery near Rome, where an old notebook of Jaussen's turned up. It contained Metoro's Polynesian chant and the Bishop's French translations. Barthel compared these texts with the four tablets that Metoro had claimed to be able to read. At first, the chants seemed just as incoherent as the Bishop had said they were—but, thanks to Barthel's code-cracking abilities, certain meanings emerged. The first success came with symbols that clearly represented the sun and the moon. These symbols were always preceded by an abstract sign combining two sticks. As Barthel wrote, "Now the sun and the moon are commonly depicted in mythologies as twins, and I recalled that a Maori (i.e., Polynesian) proverb actually refers to these celestial twins with the metaphorical expression 'two sticks.' Thus the sign became my first clue to decipherment of the Easter Island script."

Soon Barthel understood why Metoro's chants had been so badly garbled. As Barthel put it, "Metoro had been in the position of a schoolboy asked to explain a university textbook. Possessing only a rudimentary knowledge of the old script, he had read some of the signs correctly but guessed wrong on most of them, so that his over-all translation of the text was meaningless."

Barthel discovered that the Easter Island script was, as he had guessed, a kind of picture writing with no phonetic aspect. Pictures of men, of tools, of waves were used to stand for those words. But the script was subtler than that. Some symbols had more than one meaning. A character of a flower meant both "flower" and "woman." The symbol for "first-born son" was that of a decorative carving and also meant "precious ornament." Sometimes there was no apparent connection between the several meanings of a symbol, except that in the Polynesian language the same sound had several meanings. For instance, the Easter Island word *pure* means both "shell" and "prayer"—and Barthel found that a symbol showing the two halves of a shell could have either meaning, depending on the way it was used in context.

The effect of the symbol writing was to make each inscription a kind of a shorthand. A trained reader, looking along a board, could reconstruct from the symbols entire sentences of prayers or hymns. Thus the writing was more of a memory aid than a true word-by-word script. Mrs. Routledge had guessed at this when she suggested "that the signs were simply aids to recollection, or for keeping count like the beads of a rosary." She compared the characters to the knots a person might tie in his handkerchief to remind him of some obligation and observed the reason why Bishop Jaussen's native informant and other Easter Islanders had gone so far afield in trying to read the boards: "It is easy to give the term for a knot in a pocket-handkerchief, but no one save the owner can say whether he wishes to remember to pay his life insurance or the date of a tea-party."

Barthel declared that all the existing boards contain religious inscriptions. He thinks that a different script, now completely lost, was used to record historical annals. The tablets, he feels, were used at religious rituals as prompting cards to help the men who recited the Polynesian myths. Thus eight symbols, which Barthel read as PU, RUTU TE PAHU, REI, KURA, ATARIKI, HENVA, TOKO RANGI, and TANE, have this meaning according to his system of expanding them into sentences:

> *Blow the shell trumpet and beat the drum*
> *For the precious ornament*
> *For the first-born son of the earth*
> *For the prop of heaven*
> *For Tane* [a Polynesian god]

No wonder Metoro, struggling to remember the lore of his childhood, could only offer disjointed fragments! He was trying

[155]

to read a complex and compressed script, but he no longer had the necessary skill and training.

Most authorities agree today, somewhat cautiously, that Thomas Barthel has successfully solved the riddle of Easter Island's "talking boards," although there are still some who refuse to accept his findings. It is our great loss that so few of the tablets survived into the present century, for if there were more, particularly some historical records, we might be able to settle the basic mystery of Easter Island: where did its civilization come from?

Nobody thinks that a highly developed culture simply sprang into being of its own accord on this lonely, isolated island. One theory identifies Easter Island as the wreckage of a lost continent which has been called Lemuria, supposedly drowned by some great catastrophe thousands of years ago. This is an exciting and attractive notion, unfortunately not borne out by the geological facts. Easter Island, as Alfred Métraux has noted, "is plainly a typical volcanic island of recent origin, formed by a series of eruptions originating on the floor of the ocean. Soundings have revealed a depth of 1,770 fathoms 20 miles from its coast."

Others believe that the Polynesians came eastward out of China (the Heine-Geldern theory) or India (the Hevesy theory). The chief evidence for this is the resemblance of the Easter Island characters to some characters of Chinese or Indus Valley script. But the Indus Valley is 15,000 miles by land and sea from Easter Island, and its civilization is separated in time by thousands of years from that of the carvers of the "talking boards."

A more conservative theory, accepted by most authorities, is that Easter Island was settled by seafarers from the Polynesian islands farther to the west. A phrase from Barthel's deciphered tablets seems to back this idea. The phrase is, "Then they addressed their prayers to the god of Rangitea." Rangitea is one of the Friendly Islands, 1,500 miles west of Easter Island.

But if the Easter Islanders came from islands farther to the west—as their own legends seem to claim—why has the Easter Island writing never been found on any of the Polynesian islands? Were all the tablets destroyed except on remote Easter Island? Or did the Easter Islanders invent their own script without influence from their cousins of the western isles?

The most unorthodox and most carefully worked out theory is that of Thor Heyerdahl of Norway, who rejects all ideas that the Easter Islanders came from the west, whether from Polynesia, China, or India. Heyerdahl believes that Easter Island and all the other islands of the Pacific were peopled with emigrants from Peru, who floated westward on rafts more than a thousand years ago. His idea is linked to those myths of bearded white-skinned gods that were so mysteriously prevalent in the great Indian civilizations of Middle America. The Incas of Peru had a myth almost exactly parallel to the Aztec one of Quetzalcoatl and the Mayan one of Kukulcan. The Inca equivalent of these figures was called Viracocha or, according to Heyerdahl, Kon-Tiki Viracocha. Heyerdahl wrote that the Incas told the Spaniards

of a race of white gods which had lived there before the Incas themselves became rulers. These vanished architects were described as wise, peaceful instructors, who had originally come from the north, long ago in the morning of time, and had taught the Incas' primitive forefathers architecture and agriculture as well as manners and customs. They were unlike other Indians in having white skins and long beards; they were also taller than the Incas. Finally they left Peru as suddenly as they had come; the Incas themselves took over power in the country, and the white teachers vanished forever from the coast of South America and fled westward across the Pacific.

The Quetzalcoatl-Kukulcan-Viracocha legend is so persistent in American mythology that it seems almost certain to embody a germ of historical fact. It has often been used to "prove" the presence of Roman or Phoenician or Portuguese visitors in the Americas before Columbus' voyage, or even to show that Leif Ericsson's Viking relatives may have gone into southerly waters. But Heyerdahl side-stepped such issues and concentrated not on where the bearded white strangers had come from but where they had gone.

To Polynesia, he said. To prove it, Heyerdahl and five companions built a raft of balsa logs in the Inca style and put themselves to sea in 1947 from the Peruvian port of Callao. They drifted 4,300 nautical miles in 101 days, following the currents westward until their raft, the *Kon-Tiki,* ran aground on the

Polynesian atoll of Raroia. Heyerdahl had demonstrated that a raft *could* drift from Peru to Polynesia; but whether rafts *had* done so in Inca times was another matter entirely.

Through archeology Heyerdahl hoped to obtain the evidence that fair-skinned wanderers from South America had founded the civilizations of the Pacific. Although his raft had passed far north of Easter Island, he decided to begin his work there, since that island had so many tempting mysteries to unravel. In 1955 and 1956 an expedition headed by Heyerdahl worked at Easter Island and recovered a great deal of data about the origins of that strange culture.

Heyerdahl's work was careful and responsible. Yet one has to take his findings with the well-known grain of salt. He is a man who began with a theory and went looking for evidence to prove it, and that is not the method of scientific archeology. The temptation is too great, in some cases, to shape one's findings to one's preconceived ideas. By contrast, the objective scientific archeologist does his excavating first and develops his theories later from the evidence he has unearthed.

This is not to say that Heyerdahl has deliberately distorted his evidence, or that we should sneer at any archeologist who has fixed ideas about what he wants to find. Heinrich Schliemann was a dogmatic and belligerent man who insisted in the face of all learned opinion that a certain hill in Turkey was the site of Homer's Troy, and when he dug there it turned out that he had been correct. Heyerdahl, too, may have found the answers to Easter Island's enigmas—but until later expeditions have gone over the same territory, we are entitled to be slightly uneasy about his findings.

Heyerdahl has suggested that there were *three* waves of immigration to Easter Island. First, about A.D. 400 or even earlier, came Peruvian Indians aboard balsa rafts. "The people who first reached Easter Island," he wrote,

must obviously have come from an area where stone quarrying rather than wood carving was in vogue. The trees were cut to give access to solid rock. These first settlers arrived as expert masons with a highly developed technique of shaping enormous blocks of hard basalt in such a way that their visible parts could . . . fit together so closely that not a knife's blade could be inserted between them. This intricate form of megalithic masonry was unknown on the thousands of other islands further west in the Pacific, and is equalled in quality, style, and technique only by the specialized masonry characteristic of ancient Peru, on the continent which is Easter Island's nearest neighbor to the east.

Carbon-14 datings have given A.D. 380 as a time near the establishment of this first settlement. The Easter Islanders of that day built huge stone platforms and erected statues on them, but these were entirely different from the *ahu* and statues that are famous today. The Heyerdahl expedition discovered kneeling and squatting stone figures of a wholly distinct type in these early strata. They were unlike anything found on Easter Island or elsewhere in the Pacific, but—so Heyerdahl insisted—they bore resemblances to stonework from the pre-Inca settlement of Tiahuanaco in the Peruvian highlands.

About A.D. 1100, this early Easter Island civilization collapsed, and the altars and temples were abandoned. But after a gap of many years there appeared what Heyerdahl called the Middle Period culture. These people built the *ahu* and the giant stone statues, which were ancestor-figures. They, too, were Peruvians, Heyerdahl thought, judging by the evidence of their houses— thick-walled circular dwellings of stone and boat-shaped ones of sturdy reeds, both following Peruvian styles and alien to the true Polynesian cultures.

While this statue-building civilization was at its peak, Polynesians began to arrive, sailing eastward from their island homes. Since the Heyerdahl theory holds that these people too were descendants of Peruvians, they were relatives of the Easter Islanders. But they had lived so long in their western isles that their culture was wholly different. Heyerdahl put the date of this Polynesian infiltration at about A.D. 1400.

It was a peaceful invasion at first; the Polynesians settled among the Easter Islanders and adopted their ways, helping them with their vast engineering tasks. But then war broke out. An authentic island tradition tells of a civil war between two factions called the "Long Ears" and the "Short Ears," the Long Ears being the original builders of the stone statues and the Short Ears a subordinate group that worked patiently for many years but finally rebelled. In this conflict the Long Ears were almost completely exterminated, and the Short Ears tipped over many of their great statues. The traditional time of this war was twelve generations ago, or about three hundred years by Heyerdahl's reckoning. The climactic battle was said to have taken place on the peninsula of Poike, where the Short Ears pushed an ambushed group of Long Ears into a brushwood pyre and buried them in a ditch. Heyerdahl wrote:

The huge sand-filled Poike ditch was long thought by Europeans to be a natural formation, and little credit was given to the tradition of the pyre until the ditch was recently examined by excavation. It proved to be the elaborate work of man, and all along its length were carbon and ashes from an extensive pyre, which radio-carbon analysis dated to approximately A.D. 1676, which concurs perfectly with the vivid native memories.

The stone quarries were abandoned after the triumph of the Short Ears. No more statues were constructed. The island's civilization was shattered. But the Short Ears who now were the masters quarreled among themselves and with the small contingent of surviving Long Ears. Statue after statute fell in a bitter war of destruction that lasted until the middle of the nineteenth century.

Heyerdahl feels that the evidence is overwhelmingly on the side of his theory. He has proven that rafts can safely reach the Pacific islands from Peru; he points to such Peruvian culture features as the use of earplugs (the Long Ears' origin), the early mastery of stonework, and the design of houses; he cites the generally fair-skinned appearance of the Easter Islanders as a confirmation of the Viracocha story. "The links between the founders of the earlier Easter Island cultures and ancient Peru are becoming increasingly clear," Heyerdahl concludes. "The Inca records of their fair and long-eared predecessors who were driven from their stone quarries and extensive statuary activity at Tiahuanaco to disappear westwards into the open Pacific have too much in common with the Polynesian records on Easter Island to be ignored as mere native myth, if we take the concrete archeological and botanical evidence into account."

That evidence, though, is still being weighed. More conservative authorities have reservations about it. The chief spokesman for this group is Alfred Métraux, the French anthropologist. He feels that the Easter Islanders are Polynesians who found their way eastward, not Peruvians who drifted westward.

Métraux does not deny that the prevailing ocean currents could carry Peruvian rafts to the Pacific islands, and probably did, now and then. But he is skeptical toward most of Heyerdahl's ideas, beginning with the basic one of the Peruvian ancestry of the Polynesians. He notes that the Pacific islands contain numerous cultivated plants from Asia and that the Polynesian language seems related to the Indonesian languages, indicating that the origin of the Polynesians lies in the west, not in Peru to the east.

He fails to find any resemblance between the stonework of Easter Island and that of Peru. Studying pre-Inca walls at Cuzco, Métraux found that they "were constructed, without mortar, of splendidly polished blocks of stone, some of which fit together with astonishingly neat tenon and mortise joints." Three burial platforms on Easter Island superficially resemble this style, but

the resemblance between the two building techniques is deceptive, because the Easter Islanders have used relatively thin slabs to face coarse rubble walls, while the Cuzco masons boldly squared solid blocks of stone. If Indians experienced in stone-masonry had imported their art into Easter Island, it is hardly likely that they would have applied it to a type of building of which they had no equivalent in their homeland and would have failed to erect temples on the model of those at Tiahuanaco, Pucara, Cuzco, and other famous sites in Peru and Bolivia.

On the question of the "talking boards," Heyerdahl thinks the script was brought to the island by its original population of Peruvians and even identifies two of the symbols as South American creatures, a puma and a condor. But no such writing has ever been found in Peru, where unusual desert conditions would preserve even wood or textiles for thousands of years. More than that: no writing of *any* sort seems to have been in use in Peru. Heyerdahl would have us believe, then, that the Peruvians brought to Easter Island the art of writing which they had never managed to invent in their homeland, and Métraux finds this unlikely.

He admits the common use of earplugs but points out that Peru and Easter Island are not the only places in the world where such insertions in the ear lobes were employed. Métraux is puzzled, in fact, not by the presence of such a Peruvian trait on Easter Island but by the absence of so many others. "I have often wondered," he writes, "why the Peruvian Indians did not preserve in the Pacific the two arts in which they excelled—pottery and weaving. . . . The list of objects and techniques the Peruvians are said to have spread in the Pacific seems to me very scanty in comparison with the refinement of the Peruvian civilizations disclosed to us by archaeology."

Finally, Métraux challenges Heyerdahl's "uncritical" use of the traditions related by Easter Islanders in the past few generations. One of these, basic to Heyerdahl's theories, tells of a great chief named Hoto-matu'a, who led the first settlers to the island. Heyerdahl believes that Hoto-matu'a was the Peruvian chief who discovered Easter Island about A.D. 300. He bases this, apparently, mostly on a version of the legend collected in 1886 by the American seaman W. J. Thomson. This version says that Hoto-matu'a came "from a group of islands lying toward the rising sun." Métraux wonders if this can really be an authoritative text that has suffered no distortion while being handed down from father to son for sixteen centuries. And he observes that Thomson's chief source for the legend was a Tahitian who had settled on Easter Island only nine years before his visit, and who had occasionally told other questioners that Hoto-matu'a had come from the *west*.

Heyerdahl is remarkably convincing as he sets up his theories—but Métraux is just as convincing when he knocks them down. The Norwegian's excavations on Easter Island have revealed much that was unknown before and have helped to fill in many blanks in the island's history. It seems clear now that Easter Island was settled nearly two thousand years ago and had a succession of distinct cultures, which Heyerdahl has identified with precision. But where he parts company from most of the orthodox archeologists and anthropologists is in his insistence on the Peruvian origin of the early cultures of the island. The general belief is that each of the culture levels represents a Polynesian settlement and that the Polynesians themselves came not from Peru but from some Asian source.

More work is needed, and further expeditions are in the planning stage. The question of origins remains open. No one denies the possibility of occasional Peruvian visits to Easter Island, but few can accept the idea that they are the founders of the island culture. Perhaps some excavator a few years hence will uncover a cache of forgotten "talking boards" which, when deciphered, will shed new light on Easter Island's history, or possibly some undeniably Peruvian level of occupation will come to light.

Since Jacob Roggeveen landed there in 1722, men have been arguing heatedly about this strange little island. Though many of its mysteries are mysteries no more, it still holds a hornet's nest of riddles. We can look to the archeologists of tomorrow to compel that enigmatic dot of land in the Pacific to yield up the last of its secrets, perchance to reveal time-shrouded clues to the birth of civilization in the Pacific world.

Ancient cities of the Holy Land, in relation to Jericho.

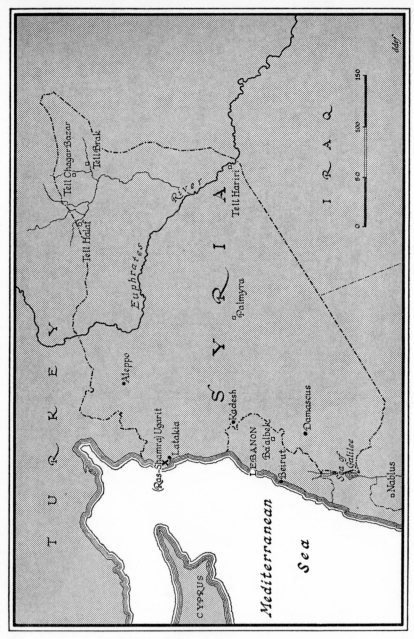

The ancient Eastern Mediterranean coast, showing Ugarit and
surrounding sites.

Ancient China, showing the Shang Empire in relation to modern cities.

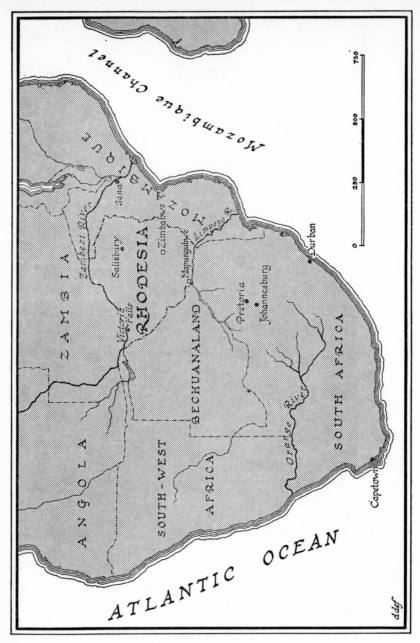

Zimbabwe and Mapungubwe, shown in relation to modern Southern
Africa.

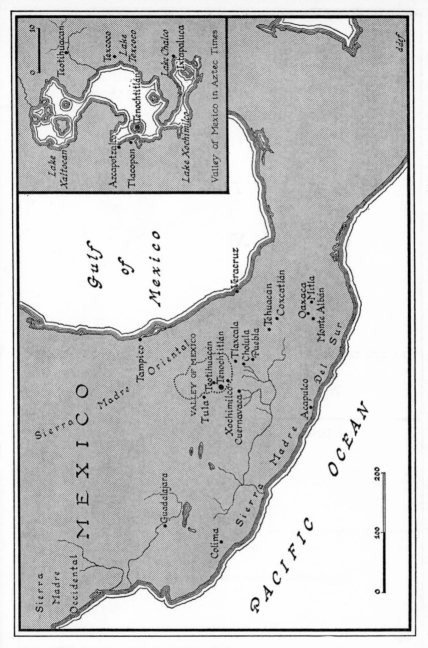

Ancient cities of Mexico; Valley of Mexico and its sites shown in
insert.

[169]

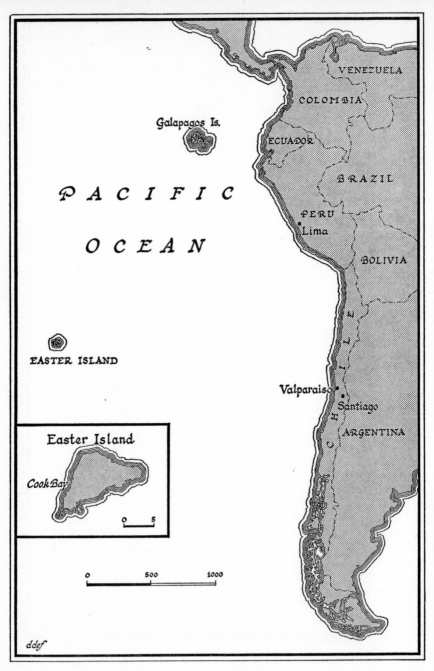

Easter Island, shown in respect to the South American coast.

Selected Bibliography

◧◧◧◧◧◧◧◧◧◧◧◧◧◧◧◧◧◧◧◧◧◧◧◧◧◧◧◧◧◧◧◧◧◧

JERICHO

ALBRIGHT, WILLIAM FOXWELL: *The Archaeology of Palestine,* revised edition. Harmondsworth, England: Penguin Books, 1960.

GRAY, JOHN: *The Canaanites.* London: Thames & Hudson, 1964; New York: Frederick Praeger, 1964.

HARDING, G. LANKESTER: *The Antiquities of Jordan.* London: Lutterworth Press, 1959.

KELLER, WERNER: *The Bible as History.* Translated by William Neil. New York: Morrow, 1956.

KELSO, JAMES L.: "The Ghosts of Jericho." *National Geographic Magazine,* Volume C, Number 6, December 1951.

KENYON, KATHLEEN M.: "Ancient Jericho." *Scientific American,* Volume 190, November 4, April 1954.

———: *Digging Up Jericho.* New York: Frederick Praeger, 1957.

——— and A. DOUGLAS TUSHINGHAM: "Jericho Gives Up Its Secrets." *National Geographic Magazine,* Volume CIV, Number 6, December 1953.

WARREN, CHARLES: *Underground Jerusalem.* London: Richard Bentley, 1876.

RAS SHAMRA–UGARIT

ALBRIGHT, WILLIAM FOXWELL: *op. cit.*

BACON, EDWARD: *Digging For History.* New York: John Day, 1961.

DIRINGER, DAVID: *Writing: Its Origins and Early History.* New York: Frederick Praeger, 1962.

DOBLHOFER, ERNST: *Voices In Stone: The Decipherment of Ancient Scripts and Writings.* Translated by Mervyn Savill. New York: Viking, 1961.

GINSBERG, H. L.: "Ugaritic Studies and the Bible." *The Biblical Archaeologist,* Volume VIII, Number 2, May 1945.

[171]

GRAY, JOHN: *op. cit.*

HARDEN, DONALD: *The Phoenicians.* London: Thames & Hudson, 1962; New York: Frederick Praeger, 1962.

NOSS, JOHN B.: *Man's Religions,* third edition. New York: Macmillan, 1963.

PRITCHARD, JAMES B., editor: *Ancient Near Eastern Texts Relating to the Old Testament,* second edition, revised. Princeton, N.J.: Princeton University Press, 1955. See particularly "Ugaritic Myths, Epics, and Legends," translated by H. L. Ginsberg.

SCHAEFFER, CLAUDE F. A.: "A New Alphabet of the Ancients is Unearthed." *National Geographic Magazine,* Volume LVIII, Number 4, October 1930.

————: *Cuneiform Texts of Ras Shamra.* London: Oxford University Press, 1939.

————: "The Oldest Alphabet." Articles from *The Illustrated London News,* November 2, 1929, and November 29, 1930, reprinted in Leo Deuel, editor: *The Treasures of Time.* Cleveland and New York: World, 1961.

SILVERBERG, ROBERT: *Akhnaten: The Rebel Pharaoh.* Philadelphia: Chilton, 1964.

————: *Empires in the Dust.* Philadelphia: Chilton, 1963.

————: *Lost Cities and Vanished Civilizations.* Philadelphia: Chilton, 1962.

SHANG

BACON, EDWARD: *op. cit.*

CREEL, HERRLEE GLESSNER: *The Birth of China.* London: Jonathan Cape, 1936; New York: Frederick Ungar, 1954.

————: *Studies in Early Chinese Culture.* Wakefield, Mass.: American Council of Learned Societies, 1938.

GILES, HERBERT A.: *A Chinese Biographical Dictionary.* Shanghai: Kelly and Walsh, 1898; New York: Paragon, 1964.

LI CHI: *The Beginnings of Chinese Civilization.* Seattle: University of Washington Press, 1957.

MENZIES, JAMES M.: "The Culture of the Shang Dynasty." Washington, D.C.: Smithsonian Institution Annual Report, 1931.

SILVERBERG, ROBERT: *The Great Wall of China.* Philadelphia: Chilton, 1965.

————: *Man Before Adam.* Philadelphia: Macrae Smith, 1964.

WATSON, WILLIAM: *China.* New York: Frederick Praeger, 1961.

WILLETS, WILLIAM: *Chinese Art.* Harmondsworth, England: Penguin Books, 1958; New York: George Braziller, 1958.

ZIMBABWE

BACON, EDWARD, editor: *Vanished Civilizations of the Ancient World.* New York: McGraw-Hill, 1963. See section "City of Black Gold" by Roger Summers.

DAMES, M. L., translator: *The Book of Duarte Barbosa.* London: The Hakluyt Society, 1918.

DAVIDSON, BASIL: *Old Africa Rediscovered.* London: Gollancz, 1959.

——: *The African Past.* London: Longmans Green, 1964; Boston: Little Brown, 1964.

HARDEN, DONALD, *op. cit.*

SCHIFFERS, HEINRICH: *The Quest for Africa.* Translated by Diana Pike. New York: Putnam, 1957.

MEXICO

BANCROFT, HUBERT HOWE: *The Native Races of the Pacific States* (five volumes). New York: D. Appleton, 1875–76.

CASO, ALFONSO: "Monte Albán, Richest Archeological Find in America." *National Geographic Magazine,* Volume LXII, Number 4, October 1932.

COE, MICHAEL D.: *Mexico.* New York: Frederick Praeger, 1962.

——: "The Chinampas of Mexico." *Scientific American,* Volume 211, Number 1, July 1964.

DÍAZ DEL CASTILLO, BERNAL: *The True History of the Conquest of New Spain* (five volumes). Translated and edited by Alfred Percival Maudslay. London: The Hakluyt Society, 1908.

——: *The Discovery and Conquest of Mexico* (one-volume abridgment of the above). New York: Farrar, Straus and Cudahy, 1956.

DRUCKER, PHILIP, and ROBERT F. HEIZER: "Gifts for the Jaguar God." *National Geographic Magazine,* Volume CX, Number 3, September 1956.

—— and ROBERT J. SQUIER: *Excavations at La Venta, Tabasco, 1955.* Washington, D.C.: Smithsonian Institution Bureau of American Ethnology Bulletin 170, 1959.

DURÁN, FRAY DIEGO: *The Aztecs: The History of the Indies of New Spain.* Translated and edited by Doris Heydan and Fernando Horcasitas. New York: Orion Press, 1964.

FUENTES, PATRICIA DE, editor: *The Conquistadors: First-person Accounts of the Conquest of Mexico.* New York: Orion Press, 1963.

JOSEPHY, ALVIN M., JR.: *The American Heritage Book of Indians.* New York: American Heritage Publishing Co., 1961.

López de Gómara, Francisco: *Cortés: The Life of the Conqueror by His Secretary.* Translated and edited by Lesley Byrd Simpson. Berkeley and Los Angeles: University of California Press, 1964.

MacNeish, Richard S.: "The Origins of New World Civilization." *Scientific American,* Volume 211, Number 5, November 1964.

Prescott, William Hickling: *The Conquest of Mexico.* New York: Modern Library, n.d.

Silverberg, Robert: *Home of the Red Man: Indian North America Before Columbus.* Greenwich, Conn.: New York Graphic Society, 1963.

———: *The Old Ones: Indians of the American Southwest.* Greenwich, Conn.: New York Graphic Society, 1965.

Stirling, Matthew W.: "Discovering the New World's Oldest Dated Work of Man." *National Geographic Magazine,* Volume LXXVI, Number 2, August 1939.

———: "Great Stone Faces of the Mexican Jungle." *National Geographic Magazine,* Volume LXXVIII, Number 3, September 1940.

Vaillant, George C.: *The Aztecs of Mexico.* Harmondsworth, England: Penguin Books, 1950.

———: "History and Stratigraphy in the Valley of Mexico." Washington, D.C.: Smithsonian Institution Annual Report, 1938.

EASTER ISLAND

Bacon, Edward, editor: *Vanished Civilizations, op. cit.* See section "Navel of the World" by Thor Heyerdahl.

Barthel, Thomas S.: "The 'Talking Boards' of Easter Island." *Scientific American,* Volume 198, Number 6, June 1958.

Beaglehole, John C.: *The Exploration of the Pacific.* London: Black, 1947.

Heyerdahl, Thor: *Aku-Aku: The Secret of Easter Island.* New York: Rand McNally, 1958.

———: *American Indians in the Pacific.* New York: Rand McNally, 1952.

———: *Kon-Tiki: Across the Pacific by Raft.* New York: Rand McNally, 1950.

———, and Edwin N. Ferdon, Jr.,: *Archaeology of Easter Island.* Santa Fe: School of American Research and the Museum of New Mexico, 1961; New York: Rand McNally.

Métraux, Alfred: *Easter Island, a Stone-Age Civilization of the Pacific,* New York: Oxford University Press, 1957.

————: "Easter Island." Washington, D. C.: Smithsonian Institution Annual Report, 1944.

————: *Ethnology of Easter Island.* Honolulu: Bernice P. Bishop Museum, 1940.

ROUTLEDGE, KATHERINE SCORESBY: *The Mystery of Easter Island.* London: Sifton Praed, 1919.

SUGGS, ROBERT C.: *Lords of the Blue Pacific.* Greenwich, Conn.: New New York Graphic Society, 1962.

Index

ROBERT SILVERBERG

Robert Silverberg specializes in the literary exploration of ancient worlds. His prize-winning *Lost Cities and Vanished Civilizations* took thousands of readers to Thebes, Carthage, Pompeii, Troy, Babylon, Machu Picchu, and Knossos. His *Sunken History: The Story of Underwater Archaeology* was a Junior Literary Guild Selection. In *Empires in the Dust,* he brought to life such ancient civilizations as those of the Phoenicians, the Etruscans, the Incas, and the dwellers of the Indus Valley. In *Akhnaten, The Rebel Pharaoh,* he recalled the life and times of the first temporal ruler ever to lead his people toward the worship of a single God.